METEOR I
VS
V1 FLYING BOMB

1944

DONALD NIJBOER

First published in Great Britain in 2012 by Osprey Publishing,
Midland House, West Way, Botley, Oxford, OX2 0PH, UK
44-02 23rd Street, Suite 219, Long Island City, NY 11101, USA

E-mail: info@ospreypublishing.com

Osprey Publishing is part of the Osprey Group

A CIP catalogue record for this book is available from the British Library

Print ISBN: 978 1 84908 706 3
PDF ebook ISBN: 978 1 84908 707 0
ePub ebook ISBN: 978 1 78200 301 4

Edited by Tony Holmes
Cover artworks and battlescene by Gareth Hector
Three-views, cockpit, gunsight, He 111, launch pad and armament scrap
views by Jim Laurier
Index by Alan Thatcher
Typeset in ITC Conduit and Adobe Garamond
Map by Bounford.com
Originated by PDQ Digital Media Solutions, Suffolk
Printed in China through Bookbuilders

12 13 14 15 16   10 9 8 7 6 5 4 3 2 1

Osprey Publishing is supporting the Woodland Trust, the UK's leading
woodland conservation charity, by funding the dedication of trees.

www.ospreypublishing.com

Acknowledgements

I would like to thank Phil Osborn, Eddie Creek, Peter Arnold, Steve Bond,
Christopher Shores, Graham Pitchfork, Phil Wilkinson, Brett Stolle and my
lovely partner Janet Walker for all their help in producing this volume.

Editor's note

For ease of comparison between types, UK imperial measurements are used
throughout this book; German metric measurements are given with imperial
equivalents in parentheses. The following data will help in converting the
imperial measurements to metric:

1 mile = 1.6km
1 yard = 0.9m
1ft = 0.3m
1in = 2.54cm/25.4mm
1hp = 0.74kW
1lb = 0.45kg
1 gallon (UK) = 4.5 litres

Meteor I cover art

On 4 August 1944 RAF fighters downed 37 V1s, and two of them were
credited to Meteor Is of No. 616 Sqn. The first flying bomb credited to a jet
aircraft was claimed by Flg Off T. D. 'Dixie' Dean at 1616 hrs, but as he
describes in his combat report, it was not destroyed by cannon fire: 'At 1545
hrs I was scrambled for an anti-Diver patrol between Ashford and
Robertsbridge. Flying at 4,500ft, 340mph IAS, I saw one Diver four to five
miles southeast of Tenterden flying at 1,000ft, estimated speed of 365mph (at
1616 hrs). From two-and-a-half miles behind the Diver I dived down from
4,500ft at 470mph. Closing into attack, I found my four 20mm guns would
not fire owing to technical trouble. I then flew my Meteor alongside the Diver
for approximately 20–30 seconds. Gradually, I manoeuvred my wingtip to a
few inches under the wing of the Diver, then pulling my aircraft upwards
sharply, I turned the Diver over onto its back and sent it diving to earth
approximately four miles south of Tonbridge. Upon returning to Manston I
was informed that the Royal Observer Corps had confirmed a Diver had
crashed at the position given by me. This is the first pilotless aircraft to be
destroyed by a jet-propelled aircraft.' (Artwork by Gareth Hector)

V1 flying bomb cover art

Twenty-five days after 'Dixie' Dean's success, Flg Off Hugh Miller shot down
his first and No. 616 Sqn's last V1 at 1415 hrs on 29 August 1944. Flying in
company with two Tempest Vs, Flg Off Miller recalled the combat: 'I
intercepted a Diver just north of Ashford. Two Tempests were seen 600 yards
behind it. Both fired but no strikes were observed. Owing to the Tempests
flying line astern of the Diver, I was forced to make a beam attack from port. I
fired three two-second bursts at 100 yards. Strikes were seen on the port wing.
I again attacked, this time from above and slightly behind at 400 yards. By this
time the two Tempests, still line astern, appeared to close in on the Diver. I
observed strikes from my fire and the Diver rolled over and exploded when it
hit the ground four miles southwest of Sittingbourne.' On that day RAF
fighters were credited with 23 V1s destroyed. (Artwork by Gareth Hector)

CONTENTS

INTRODUCTION

The desperation was beginning to tell. Poor weather severely curtailed all operations and only four anti-Diver patrols had been attempted since the squadron had traded its Spitfire VIIs for Gloster Meteor Is – the first jets to enter frontline service with the RAF. It was 2 August 1944. With the Allied armies firmly established in Normandy, the pilots of No. 616 Sqn were anxious to test their new secret weapon against Germany's latest aerial assault. They would not have long to wait.

In this colour image taken from a ciné film, an unidentified No. 616 Sqn pilot climbs aboard Meteor I YQ-K at Manston in August 1944. The pilot is equipped with the standard Irvin Type S-2 seat parachute. The Meteor I was not fitted with an ejection seat, and in case of an emergency pilots would have been forced to bale out of the jet the old-fashioned way. (Author's Collection)

The following day Flt Lt Mike Grave spotted his first Diver (the Allied codename for the V1 flying bomb). With throttles pushed forward, he quickly closed the gap between himself and the sleek, sinister flying machine. The V1, oblivious to its pursuer, rushed headlong towards London. With his finger firmly on the trigger, Graves slipped in behind the droning missile and fired a two-second burst. His four 20mm cannon roared into life, spitting out 100 rounds of high explosive/incendiary and semi-armour-piercing shells. The V1 seemed to shrug off the assault and continued on its path. Graves had fired too soon. From a range of 400–500 yards there was no evidence that any of his shells had hit home, and just as he manoeuvred in for a second attack a Mustang stole the show. A quick squirt of 0.50in shells from the P-51's six wing guns sent the V1 crashing to the ground. It was not the most auspicious start, but history had been made nevertheless. The world's first jet-versus-jet encounter had taken place.

Across the English Channel, the *Führer*'s strategy of vengeance was playing itself out. On 16 May 1944 he ordered an all-out missile attack on London to begin by mid-June. It was to be a massive offensive, with 1,000 ground-launched V1 flying bombs supported by aircraft-launched versions, long-range coastal artillery and bomber aircraft attacks. Codenamed *Rumpelkammer* ('Junk Room'), it was another example of Hitler's over-inflated grasp of the real military situation.

Just as the crews from No. 616 Sqn were taking to the skies, the men of *Flak-Regiment* 155(W) were frantically assembling, fuelling and launching as many V1s towards London as humanly possible. But even their efforts were not enough. It was just a matter of time before Allied troops broke out from their Normandy beachhead, and when that happened *Flak-Regiment* 155(W)'s prized launch sites from Dieppe to Calais would have to be abandoned and the assault ended.

Emerging from a heavily camouflaged underground storage facility a few miles from the French coast, *Flak-Regiment* 155(W) groundcrewmen wheel an Fi 103A-1 out into the open on a *Zubringerwagon* loading trolley prior to sliding it onto a catapult ready for launching. The transport cone attached to the front of the weapon protected the nose-mounted windmill propeller and warhead fuses. This photograph was taken during the opening phase of operations in June 1944. (Eddie Creek)

An early-production Fi 103A-1 sits on a fixed launch rail at Zempin, on the Baltic coast, in late 1943. This weapon was expended by *Flak-Regiment* 155(W) whilst the unit was undergoing intensive training on how to assemble, mount and launch a V1 successfully. (Author's Collection)

For those few short weeks in August 1944 the Allies first operational jet fighter was pitted against the world's first cruise missile. It was one of the most distinctive aerial assaults of the war, and one that exposed Germany's many faults and failures, but also its technological ingenuity. For the Allies the Gloster Meteor I was a conditional triumph, and one most pilots would say was just slightly better than the existing piston-engined fighters then in squadron service. But the piston engine had little room for expansion. The Spitfire I of the Battle of Britain was powered by a 1,030hp Rolls-Royce Merlin II engine and developed a speed of roughly 355mph. The F XIV version of 1944 was powered by a Rolls-Royce Griffon 65 engine developing 2,050hp, giving it a top speed of 450mph. In the quest for more speed another 1,000 horsepower would not equate to an additional 100mph. Piston engines had reached their point of diminishing returns. More power meant more weight for no real increase in speed. It would be the jet engine that would transform the equation with startling results.

While both the Gloster Meteor I and Messerschmitt Me 262A-1a were the world's first jet fighters to see combat during World War II, they were not, however, the first jet-powered aircraft to see action. That title goes to the Fieseler Fi 103 pulse-jet flying bomb.

Having received orders to initiate Operation *Eisbär* (Polar Bear) – the missile attacks on London – on the evening of 12 June 1944, *Flak-Regiment* 155(W)'s first V1 (*Vertgeltungswaffe* 1 – Revenge Weapon No. 1) launches were a complete flop. The second salvo, which commenced at 0350 hrs on 13 June, proved marginally more successful. Twenty minutes into the operation, at 0350 hrs near Hesdin, in northern France, a V1 stood fully fuelled and ready for launch. Its pulse-jet engine was started, and seven seconds later, having reached maximum thrust, the V1 was accelerated along a 160ft Walter launch ramp via a piston that was driven by a pulse of high-pressure steam. Reaching a speed of about 250mph by the time it left the ground, the missile attained its cruising altitude of roughly 3,000ft six minutes later. A total of ten V1s had been fired in this salvo, and four crashed immediately or shortly after takeoff. The Hesdin weapon flew on, however, and it duly became the first jet-powered craft to be tracked and viewed by Britain's defences. At 0410 hrs British radar at Swingate, near Dover, caught its first glimpse of this new form of warfare.

Defence against the V1 flying bomb fell jointly upon Anti-Aircraft (AA) Command and the newly created Air Defence of Great Britain (ADGB). Initial patrols were undertaken by 11 squadrons of fighters, which at the height of the battle were flying Tempest Vs, Spitfire IXs and XIVs, Mustang IIIs and Mosquito nightfighters.

The advent of the V1 would prove to be an ideal opportunity to test Britain's newest secret weapon – the twin-jet Gloster Meteor I. The introduction of the fighter into RAF service was somewhat premature, the first jets being essentially militarised versions of the F.9/40 prototypes powered by two Rolls-Royce W.2B/23C Welland engines and, in many ways, not combat ready. Indeed, legendary British test pilot Capt Eric Brown described the performance of the Mk I as 'pedestrian'. Compared with the high performance piston-engined fighters then in service with the RAF (the Tempest V and Spitfire XIV), the Meteor offered little in the way of superior performance. Where it excelled, however, was at low level – exactly where the V1 operated. The Meteor I was faster than any of its contemporaries at such altitudes. This was just as well, for the V1 boasted an average speed of roughly 400mph between 1,000ft and 3,000ft. At those heights the Tempest V and Spitfire XIV could make 405mph and 396mph, respectively, using 150-octane fuel. The Meteor, on the other hand, had a top speed of 410mph at sea level.

The short battle between the Meteor I and V1 in the summer of 1944 would ultimately prove to be a modest success for Britain's first jet fighter. For the Germans, it was another example of their technical prowess being frittered away through blind vengeance and obsessive false hope.

CHRONOLOGY

1936

16 January — Plt Off Frank Whittle takes out his first patent (No. 347206) for a gas turbine engine.

March — The Power Jets Company is formed with Whittle as chief engineer.

1937

12 April — Whittle U.1 type jet engine is run for the first time.

May — Germany's missile test site at Peenemünde opens.

1938

March — Air Ministry is convinced that Whittle's engine shows promise and places order for a flight engine designated W.1.

1940

3 February — Gloster Aircraft is contracted to design Britain's first jet fighter under the F.9/40 specification.

1941

January — German aircraft engine company Argus begins testing of its new pulse-jet engine.

30 April — Pulse-jet is test flown on a Gotha Go 145 biplane.

September — Initial production order for 20 Meteor fighters is placed with Gloster.

1942

27 February — Fieseler engineer Robert Lusser visits Argus, where a simple pulse-jet aircraft is sketched out, providing the genesis for the Fi 103 (V1 flying bomb).

March — Hitler demands retaliatory strikes against Britain in response to the RAF's heavy bomber attacks.

30 April — First Fi 103 is completed.

3 July — Meteor prototype F.9/40 DG202/G begins taxi trials.

August — First Rolls-Royce built W.2B/23 Welland is test flown in a converted Wellington bomber. This engine is built in small numbers and equips the Meteor I.

10 December — The first powered launch of the Fi 103 V7 takes place over the Baltic using an Fw 200 Condor.

1943

5 March — Meteor prototype DG206/G makes first flight powered by two Halford H.1 turbojets.

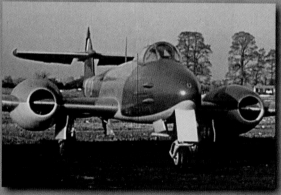

Another rare ciné film still, this time showing Meteor EE214 in the standard non-operational colour scheme of the day – Dark Green and Ocean Grey uppersurfaces and Trainer Yellow undersides. The faired-over gun ports indicated that this jet was not armed, EE214 being used as a training aircraft for pilot conversion. Most if not all the pilots in No. 616 Sqn flew either EE213 or EE214 as part of their conversion training. (Author's Collection)

1944 (handwritten)

April	Oberst Max Wachtel is appointed commander of the first V1 unit *Flak-Regiment* 155(W), the W standing for *Werfer*, or launcher.
26 October	First V1 training launch by Watchel's unit takes place.
December	Air Marshal Sir R. M. Hill, Commander-in-Chief of ADGB, is ordered to prepare a plan of defence against V1 flying bomb.
5 December	Allied aircraft begin attacks on V1 launch sites in France.

1944

12 January	First Meteor I (EE210/G) makes its maiden flight, powered by two Rolls-Royce W.2B/23C Wellands.
March	Quantity production of V1 is reached.
16 May	Hitler orders the missile attack on London, codenamed Operation *Eisbär*, to commence by mid-June.
12 June	First nine V1s are launched towards London, but none of these reach England.
13 June	Second salvo of V1s is more successful, with ten launches and four missiles reaching England. One lands in London suburb of Bethnal Green at 0418 hrs.
18 June	Gen Dwight Eisenhower, Supreme Allied Commander, rules that long-range weapon targets must take precedence over everything except the urgent requirements for the battle of Normandy.
28 June	Anti-V1 defences are increased to 1,400 barrage balloons, 376 heavy AAA guns, 576 light guns, plus 560 light guns of the RAF Regiment, and two US Army radar-directed AAA battalions.
9 July	He 111 bombers from III./KG 3 begin attacks on London with air-launched V1s.

– Polar Bear (handwritten)

20 July	First two Meteor Is (EE213/G and EE214/G – 'G' denoted that the aircraft required an armed guard at all times) are delivered to No. 616 Sqn. Unit eventually receives a total of 16 Mk Is.
3 August	V1 missile assault peaks with 316 launches, of which 220 reach London. By mid-August Allied ground forces are across the River Seine and threatening all V1 launch sites.
4 August	Flg Off T. D. Dean of No. 616 Sqn brings down the unit's first V1. It is not shot down but tipped out of the sky.
29 August	Flg Off H. Miller of No. 616 Sqn shoots down the unit's last V1.
1 September	Last French-based V1 is launched at 0400 hrs.

This Fi 103A-1 was found abandoned at a launch site near a Ninth Air Force airfield in northern France in the autumn of 1944. This was the standard version of the V1 used in the campaign against London. The two fuses have been removed from the nose of the weapon, which was subsequently transported to the USA for evaluation. (NARA)

DESIGN AND DEVELOPMENT

METEOR I

By 1944 aerodynamic advances and sheer horsepower had finally caught up with the single-seat fighter of World War II. Since 1936 engine power had virtually doubled, but the limitations of the piston engine were beginning to tell. The Hawker Tempest V was equipped with the Napier Sabre IIA, which delivered 2,180hp, the P-51H's Packard V-1650-9 developed 2,218hp and the Jumo 213 fitted in the Fw 190D was capable of 2,240hp with water methanol injection. All three fighters had top speeds in excess of 420mph, with the P-51H topping off at 487mph.

This was a remarkable achievement, but one that was limited by the increase in weight and complexity of larger piston engines and the degrading properties of a spinning propeller. And just as some of the world's largest piston engines ever built were about to be bench tested, jet technology matured to the point where the horsepower equivalent produced by a turbo jet matched, and in some cases exceeded, most frontline piston engines.

Jet engines were also relatively simple to construct, and did not require the heavy machinery needed for large liquid or radial air-cooled engines. They were also lightweight and relatively inexpensive, and while early fuel consumption was high, that improved as the new technology moved forward. It was in this transition period that the Gloster Meteor was born.

The hard work of developing British jet technology began in 1928 with Plt Off Frank Whittle. His ideas of using a gas turbine to produce a jet of hot air in order to propel an aircraft were submitted to the British Air Ministry in 1929. Early reaction was disappointing, with civil servants declaring Whittle's ideas impractical. Undaunted, he forged ahead with his research, and on 16 January 1930 he took out his first patent (No. 347206) for a gas turbine.

In 1935, with little or no interest from the British government, Whittle managed to obtain some private financial support to build his first jet engine. In January of that year he submitted his design to the British Thompson-Houston Co., and in April the following year his WU (Whittle Unit) type engine was ready for bench testing. The new engine was a considerable leap forward, and consisted of a single-stage, centrifugal, double-sided compressor, and was driven by a directly coupled single-stage turbine. As air was drawn into the large U-shaped cylinder, it was mixed with fuel, ignited and fed directly into the turbine. The result was super hot gases being ejected from the long jet pipe.

Whittle's WU engine turned out to be a fiery beast. When bench tested for the first time on 12 April 1937, it seemed to have a mind of its own. Every time the fuse was lit it kept surging uncontrollably, speeding up to 8,000rpm even when the throttle was chopped. Fuel pooling in the combustion chamber caused the engine to run

As the first British jet engine to be fitted in an aircraft, the W.1, built by British Thompson-Houston, provided the thrust needed to get the Gloster E.28/29 prototype into the air on 15 May 1941. Whittle's design utilised a simple double-sided centrifugal compressor, reverse-flow annular combustion chambers and a water-cooled axial-flow turbine section – the latter was subsequently changed to an air-cooled design. (ww2images.com)

wildly, and it did not stop until this fuel was completely burned. Combustion in the WU engine was also considered poor – so bad in fact that smoke and flames would scream through the jet pipe, causing the curved chamber to glow red hot. Whittle would later say, 'These early tests made it clear that the combustion problem was by no means solved, and the compressor performance was far below expectations. A design change was in order.'

Whittle revised his first design and built a second unit that had a straight boiler-like combustion chamber which was fed by ten pipes from a compressor. The second engine was short lived, as Whittle describes:

> Only nine test runs were made on the second model of the experimental engine because the ninth test was brought to an end by a turbine failure that caused fairly extensive damage. For eight of these test runs the speed never exceeded about 8,500rpm, but in the last run of the series a speed of 13,000rpm was maintained for half an hour, at the end of which the failure occurred.

A major change in the arrangement of the engine had to be made. This resulted in a new design that had ten separate combustion chambers disposed radially, with their ends lying parallel with the compressor and turbine wheels. This was the major breakthrough Whittle had been searching for, and the unit known as the U.1 became the forerunner to the W.1.

Testing began at the end of October 1938, with engine power being gradually increased until a turbine disc shredded and destroyed the unit in February 1941. By then the Air Ministry had finally been convinced that the Whittle engine was no fluke, and in March 1938 it placed the first contract for the W.1. Part of the agreement

The air intake of E.28/39 W4041 clearing shows its bifurcated form. Air from the nose intake was fed into the engine through the two ducts, which converged behind the cockpit into a plenum chamber. This aircraft survived the war and is on permanent display at the Science Museum in London. Legendary naval test pilot Eric 'Winkle' Brown performed E.28/39's last flight on 20 February 1945. He described the aircraft as a 'little beauty', which lived up to Whittle's maxim of simplicity and reliability. The machine had a sparkling performance thanks to its W.2/500 engine that delivered 1,760lb (798kg) of thrust. (Author's Collection)

Meteor I EE211/G was the second production example built, and it first flew on 16 April 1944. Retained by Gloster, the jet was transferred to RAE Farnborough for extensive trials. It is seen here at the latter airfield complete with airflow tufts attached to the port wing and engine nacelle. The tufts were used by engineers when studying airflow patterns around the inner wing and engine nacelle. The aircraft was transferred from Gloster to Maintenance Command in April 1946 and given ground instructional serial 5927M. (Author's Collection)

required the engine to be similar to the U.1 in aerodynamic and thermodynamic design, with a sharp focus on lightness. Unfortunately, work on the new engine progressed slowly. With the outbreak of war more money was made available to expand the project and move it forward. Finally, in March 1940, the Ministry of Aircraft Production (MAP) took over full financial responsibility for the new jet engine.

The previous month the Air Ministry had issued Britain's first contract for a jet aircraft (SB/3229). Gloster Aircraft had been chosen to meet specification E.28/39, with the second paragraph of the document clearly stating 'the primary object of this aeroplane will be to flight test the engine installation, but the design will be based on requirements for a fixed gun interceptor fighter as far as the limitations of size and weight imposed by the power unit permit'.

The design of this new aircraft was a collaboration between Frank Whittle and Gloster's designer George Carter. They envisaged a low-winged monoplane with the engine mounted behind the cockpit and equipped with a tricycle undercarriage. Air for the engine would be drawn in from the nose then passed through ducts that ran either side of the cockpit. The Gloster E.28/29 was in many ways one of the world's first technology demonstrator aircraft. Its sole purpose was to flight test Whittle's W.1 jet engine, which developed a modest 860lb of thrust. A remarkable aircraft by any standard, two examples were built (W4041 and W4046).

On 15 May 1941, W4041, piloted by Gerry Sayer, took off from Cranwell at 1945 hrs. The flight lasted just 17 minutes, but it was a historic first. Capt Eric 'Winkle' Brown, the Royal Navy's top test pilot, would have the opportunity to fly W4041 in 1944. By that time it was powered by the new W.2/500 engine, with a thrust double that of the W.1. Brown subsequently recalled:

I was flight-testing this aircraft and the jet fighter (Meteor) at Farnborough. Let me say, the first thing that struck you as a pilot was the marvellous view you had. There was no big engine sticking out in front. That was the first thing. The second was that when you got in the air there was a total lack of vibration, which you had so much of in a piston-engined aircraft. Thirdly, there was a lack of noise. There may have been a lot of noise outside, but you were sitting ahead of the jet engine, and there was virtually no noise at all. So these were the three big impressions. The acceleration on this little aeroplane [E.28/29] wasn't bad either, and considering it was a very small engine, it had remarkable performance. Eventually, the Meteor that came out not very long after [E.28/29] was a disappointment. I would class the Meteor I as a very pedestrian aircraft.

The second aircraft, W4046, first flew on 1 March 1943. This machine would crash three months later after experiencing jammed ailerons during an inverted spin from 33,000ft.

The promise of Whittle's engine pushed the Air Ministry to plan for the first operational jet fighter. Even before the first E.28/29 took shape, Specification F.9/40 was finalised in December 1940. Because the new jet engine did not have the required thrust, the fighter would have to be twin-engined. The F.9/40 was not a radical or advanced aerodynamic design. It followed accepted aircraft practices and was fairly conventional. On 7 February 1941, Gloster received an order to supply 12 'Gloster-Whittle aeroplanes' to the F.9/40 specification. Due to problems with subcontractors and production delays with the new W.2B engine, construction of the new Meteor prototypes was slow and protracted during the summer of 1941.

On 26 June 1942 the first Meteor prototype, DG202/G, fitted with W.2B engines, was used for taxiing trials only, and not cleared for flight. Finally, on 5 March 1943, Meteor prototype DG206/G, powered by a pair of Halford H.1 turbojets, flew for the first time. With taxiing trials finished and the first flight completed, work on the remaining six F.9/40 prototypes continued, albeit at a very slow and frustrating pace.

On 1 April it was reported that DG202 was 'practically finished, awaiting W.2/500 engines. There is no promise for the engines owing to the fact that one has blown up on the test bench.' DG203 'is in practically the same state as DG202'. DG204 is 'equipped with Metro-Vickers axial flow engines. There is a fair amount of work which cannot be done until after the undercarriage is fitted.' DG205 has 'W.2B engines installed. Shall be ready for engine runs three weeks from today.' Of the rest, DG206 was the only flying aircraft, with DG207 and DG208 both awaiting modification. Engine problems slowed development considerably, with official confidence having been shaken when the W.2B's impeller repeatedly burst at high speed. This fault was eventually remedied with imported impellers from General Electric, who in 1941 had built its own jet engine based on Whittle's design. Fortunately for the programme, Rolls-Royce was called upon to take over development and production of the W.2B engine.

As flight testing continued, construction of the new G.41A Meteor I fighter was gaining momentum (the initial production order was issued in September 1941). Twenty Mk Is (Serials EE210–EE229) were under construction as an initial order, and the first of these, EE210, was completed but not flown until January 1944. Powered by two Rolls-Royce W.2B/23C Welland I engines developing 1,700lb of thrust each, the new Mk I had a maximum speed of 415mph at 10,000ft. In reality the Meteor I was simply a militarised version of the F.9/40 prototype. It differed little in general appearance, both internally and externally. There were several minor airframe refinements, including a clear-view transparent canopy, and it was fully armed with four Hispano Mk III 20mm cannons. Of the 20 Mk Is built, only 16 were delivered to the RAF (EE213 to EE222 and EE224 to EE229).

In July 1944 Spitfire VII-equipped No. 616 Sqn, based at Culmhead, in Somerset, was duly chosen to become the first Allied unit to fly jet fighters operationally. Royal Canadian Air Force pilot Flg Off Bill 'Mac' Mackenzie recalled the squadron's early, non-high tech, introduction to jet flight:

> One day this gorgeous, clapped-out Oxford arrived at flight dispersal and the 'Old Man' [Sqn Ldr Leslie Watts] announced that this was to be our training aircraft – we were all going to become twin-engined pilots! A couple of days later the CO and I flew down to Farnborough where we were to see our new aircraft. We entered the hangar, going through three checkpoints where service police checked our ID cards and demanded signatures. I had my first look at the 'thing' sitting there, looking like a dragon with two big empty eyes.

When the Meteor I entered service it was not a sparkling performer. For all its cutting-edge technology, the Gloster jet was just 21mph faster than the Spitfire F XIV at 13,000ft, and its rate of climb was considerably inferior. Ironically, when the Meteor was first considered for production the RAF had no requirement for such a fighter. In early 1943 MAP produced comparative performance curves for both the Meteor and the proposed Spitfire F 21. These showed that the Meteor I had a higher maximum speed at low and high altitude, but its rate of climb was inferior and range meagre at best.

Where the Meteor I excelled was as a short-range daylight home defence interceptor, operating against low-flying targets. When the V1 attack started in June 1944 the Meteor was ideally suited to the task. Its trump card was its high speed at low level. The best RAF piston-engined fighters of the time – the Spitfire F XIV, Tempest V and Mustang III – could not reach 400mph at 2,000ft (the V1 operated at between 1,000ft and 3,000ft). The best they could manage, with 150-octane fuel, was 366mph for the Spitfire F XIV, 386mph for the Tempest V and 390mph for the Mustang III, but those speeds could only be maintained for short periods. The Meteor, on the other hand, could cruise at 410mph, making it the ideal V1 interceptor.

The Meteor achieved many firsts. It was the first operational jet fighter in Allied service, and it was also the first to be put into mass production. But, more importantly, it would make history as the world's first jet fighter to down another jet-powered aircraft. This event occurred on 4 August 1944 when Flg Off T. D. Dean (flying EE216/YQ-E) used the wingtip of his Meteor to flip a V1 on to its back, sending the missile diving to earth. No. 616 Sqn's diarist noted 'The first flying bomb was destroyed by a jet-propelled aircraft. This note in the squadron history, and indeed aviation history, can be recorded by Flg Off Dean.'

METEOR I

41ft 3in

13ft 0in

43ft 0in

V1 FLYING BOMB

The V1 flying bomb was an example of a weapon created not for a desired military specification (tactical or strategic), but one that evolved out of circumstance, timing, simplicity and vengeance. What the V1 and Gloster Meteor shared in terms of technology was only skin deep. While both were jet-powered aircraft, the Meteor was obviously far more sophisticated. The V1, on the other hand, was powered by the most basic of pulse-jet engines, and was a crude and inaccurate area-bombardment weapon. In terms of technological development, the V1 could have been in service in time for the Battle of Britain, but fortunately for the British, Germany had no need for a pilotless flying bomb in the summer of 1940.

The idea for the V1 could be traced back to World War I. Just as the many different fighting roles for aircraft were being developed (fighter, bomber, fighter-bomber, reconnaissance etc.) the concept of a pilotless flying bomb was being considered as well. In 1915 the Sperry Gyroscope Co. began to experiment with 'aerial torpedoes' using gyroscopes to guide a flying machine to its target. After the war the British conducted similar trials with the Larynx flying bomb in 1927. Thirteen years later, with RAF Bomber Command unable to inflict any damage on the German war machine, the Miles Aircraft Company proposed an unmanned, radio-controlled, Gypsy Major-engined aircraft that could carry a 1,000lb bomb over an estimated range of 400 miles. Given the name Hoopla, a mock-up was built, but the Air Ministry showed no interest. Ironically, MAP considered the idea of an unmanned bomb 'beneath contempt'. The mock-up, however, was retained until 1948.

Both Larynx and Hoopla proved that the idea for such a weapon was far ahead of the technology then available to make them effective. Even the V1 in its final form was both unreliable and inaccurate, but it did show that the unmanned flying bomb was a viable weapon, and it would be the first in a long line of new weapons that would ultimately culminate in today's highly effective cruise missile.

OPPOSITE
Meteor I EE216/G was the mount of Flg Off T. D. Dean on 4 August 1944 when he claimed the world's first jet-versus-jet victory. With his cannons jammed, Dean flew alongside the V1 and used his wingtip to roll the missile onto its back, sending the weapon earthward until it crashed approximately four miles south of Tonbridge. Initially assigned to the RAE in the spring of 1944, E216/G was transferred to No. 616 Sqn in July of that year. Replaced by a Meteor III in early 1945, it was passed on to No. 1335 Conversion Unit at Molesworth, where the aircraft was used in the training of Meteor pilots for frontline squadrons. The veteran aircraft was struck off charge in January 1946 and subsequently scrapped.

The Fi 103 would not have been possible without the pulse-jet engine. A reciprocal powerplant was out of the question, and the much more sophisticated jet engine would have been too expensive to build and a complete waste of vital metals and man hours for just a one-off flight. The simple pulse-jet was the perfect choice, but it did have its drawbacks. The engine's life span was measured in hours, but in the case of the V1 that did not matter. (Author's Collection)

Pulse-jet research began in Germany in 1928, with Paul Schmidt being a pioneer in this field. He quickly realised that the simple, inexpensive pulse-jet would be the ideal powerplant for a missile. In 1935 he approached the Luftwaffe with his design, which he had conceived with the help of Prof G. Madelung. It was a design ahead of its time, and included the novel feature of a mid-fuselage air intake. However, the Luftwaffe could see no tactical use for the weapon and rejected it as 'technically dubious'. The idea of pilotless aircraft was not a new concept, and there were many others who saw new roles for this type of machine.

In a separate venture, Dr Fritz Gosslau of Argus Motor Works developed the FZG 43 (*Flakzielgerät* 43, Anti-aircraft Target Device 43). This was a remote-controlled model aeroplane for use as a target drone for German flak crews. In October 1939 Argus expanded its idea and came up with *Fernfeuer* (Deep Fire). This was a larger radio-controlled aircraft that could carry a one-ton bombload. Controlled by a piloted version of the same design, it would deliver its bomb and then return to base. It was an intriguing concept, and one the Luftwaffe was open to, but by 1940–41 the idea of an area-bombardment weapon was no longer a priority.

The limited success of the V1 centred on the pulse-jet engine. Without it the weapon would not have been possible. As early as 1908 the first primitive pulse-jets had been studied, but they would not reach maturity until the 1940s. The pulse-jet represents the most basic jet technology. It works by simply injecting fuel into a combustion chamber, mixing it with air and igniting it. The resulting explosion creates a jet of hot gases that can be directed back through an exhaust tube. If this mix is repeated quickly enough, continuous thrust is created. Early studies revealed that under ideal conditions the combustion cycle could be self-sustaining. There was also a need for a practical technique to prevent the jet thrust from blasting through the air intake at the front of the engine.

By 1941 a convergence had begun. Argus, primarily an engine manufacturer, began work on pulse-jet engine designs completely independently of Schmidt in 1939. The following year the Luftwaffe encouraged Schmidt and Argus to collaborate, even though they considered such work a low priority. Schmidt was able to produce a simple but effective shutter air intake system for the pulse-jet. His design allowed air to enter the combustion chamber through shutters at the front, and these would automatically close once the fuel air mixture detonated. All of the energy was now forced back out through the exhaust tube. A superior design, it was incorporated into the next stage of development. Argus contributed by building an innovative method of injecting atomised fuel into the combustion chamber that resulted in a stable combustion sequence.

This combination produced the Argus-Schmidt engine, which was both cheap to build and remarkably simple in design when compared with rival turbojets being built by Jumo in Germany and Power Jets in the UK. All early jet engines were not fuel efficient, and the pulse-jet was by far the worst for fuel usage. And because it was a resonating engine, the combustion detonations occurred several times per second, which meant the engine was in essence slowly tearing itself apart. In effect the V1 actually slowed down after just 15–20 minutes of flight owing primarily to the gradual disintegration of the shutters at the front of the pulse-jet. This in turn gave the RAF's piston-engined fighters their best chance of catching the high-speed missile.

Argus began to test its pulse-jet using automobiles in January 1941. On 30 April the first flight of a pulse-jet occurred when an engine was strapped to a Gotha Go 145 biplane. The Luftwaffe continued to show support while Dr Gosslau focused more and more on the idea of using the pulse-jet to power a flying bomb. But Argus was deficient in the aircraft design department. Help soon arrived when Robert Lusser, a Fieseler aircraft engineer, paid a visit to Argus on 27 February 1942. Dr Gosslau suggested that Argus and Fieseler should pool their talents and work on a viable flying bomb. He proposed an aircraft with two pulse-jets under each wing, but Lusser sketched out an even bolder concept – mount a single engine above the tail. It was during this brief meeting that the genesis of the V1 flying bomb was born.

By the end of April 1942 Lusser had completed a preliminary design known as the Fieseler P 35 Erfurt. Radio and radar guidance options were quickly rejected as a means to guide the weapons, as Allied electronic countermeasures would most certainly nullify any new system. The Germans instead turned to gyroscopes to build an inertial guidance system. The P 35 was designed to carry a half-ton warhead at a speed of 700kmh (435mph) over a distance of up to 300km (186 miles). Submitted to the Luftwaffe on 5 June 1942, the new Erfurt found a more receptive audience.

Since the Battle of Britain the strategic situation had changed. The Luftwaffe was almost fully committed to the Russian front and the Mediterranean. In March 1942 the RAF had begun systematic heavy bomber attack. The first major success for Bomber Command against a German target occurred on 28/29 March, when 234 aircraft bombed the city of Lübeck. Approximately 30 per cent of Lübeck's built-up areas were destroyed by fire. Hitler was furious and demanded retaliatory strikes against England, but the Luftwaffe's offensive bomber force in the west was anaemic at best, centring on just a handful of Do 217s and two *Staffeln* of fighter-bombers.

In January 1941 Argus Motor Works began testing its pulse-jet engine on automobiles. This was soon followed by a first flight test attached to a Gotha Go 145 primary trainer (seen here) on 30 April 1941. The results proved promising and the Luftwaffe supported further development. (Author's Collection)

It was at this time that the Wehrmacht lobbied Hitler on the premise that its A4 (V2, or *Vertgeltungswaffe* 2 – Revenge Weapon No. 2) ballistic missile could do what the Luftwaffe had failed to do during the Battle of Britain. The Luftwaffe's leadership had had enough. It was time to act, and on 19 June 1942 the flying bomb project was approved. Shortly thereafter the P 35 was renamed the Fieseler Fi 103 and codenamed *Kirschkern* (Cherry Stone). It was later given the cover name FZG 76 (*Flakzielgerät* 76).

Spurred on now by a new sense of urgency, Fieseler completed the first Fi 103 on 30 August 1942. This was followed by a new version of the Argus pulse-jet the following month, but there were problems. The high-speed test trials that followed proved to be a total failure, however, and nearly ended the programme, It was subsequently shown that these results were due to wind-tunnel test anomalies and not a major problem with the engine. As the pulse-jet tests were undertaken, the first unpowered flight was conducted from an Fw 200 Condor on 28 October 1942. It proved to be a success, with the well-designed missile proving very stable in flight. This was followed by the first powered test on 10 December 1942 of Fi 103 V7 – the V7 denoted that it was the seventh test *Vorserienzellen* (prototype pre-production) airframe.

The first powered launch of the V1 occurred on 24 December when Fi 103 V12 was propelled into the air from the top-secret Peenemünde missile test site. Reaching a speed of 500kmh (310mph), it flew for about a minute before crashing into the Baltic Sea. While the flight had been a bit of a failure, it did lead to approval of full-scale development. Keen to maintain momentum on the weapon's development, Fieseler (airframe), Argus (engine), Askania (guidance) and Walter (launch catapult system) were all involved in critical tests at this time. This in turn led to major problems owing to the inability to determine which system was responsible for any one failure. As a result, the test programme was much like the operational life of the V1 – full of crashes.

Many were caused by the pulse-jet engine, as the enormous amount of noise and vibration generated by the fuel detonating 47 times per second inside the powerplant was literally shaking the aircraft apart. The shutters in front of the pulse-jet caused most of the problems because of their tendency to disintegrate during flight. Yet despite these challenging technical issues, 84 Fi 103s had been launched – 16 from the

The first test flights of early V1 airframes were conducted at the Luftwaffe's Test Establishment at Karlshagen at Peenemünde-West. Using an Fw 200 Kondor bomber, the first non-powered flight occurred on 28 October 1942. This was followed by the first powered flight – of Fi 103 V7 (the V7 indicating that it was the seventh test airframe) – on 10 December that same year. (Eddie Creek)

Fi 103A-1

7.73m (25ft 4in)

1.42m (4ft 8in)

5.33m (17ft 6in)

air and 68 by catapult – by the end of July 1943. More worrying was the fact that only 28 of the catapult launches (from purpose-built Walter WR 2.3 *Schlitzrohrschleuder* catapults) had been successful. More problematic was the fact that none of the missiles was fitted with a full guidance system, and not one was launched at a full combat weight. In the end about a third of the V1s failed to launch, or crashed seconds after leaving the ramp.

At the heart of the V1 was its guidance system. Trials of the new Askania autopilot began in the summer of 1943. To keep the missile stable in flight, at the right altitude and going in the right direction required three different devices to work in harmony. The first was the magnetic compass, which kept the missile heading along a predetermined magnetic bearing, whilst a pair of gyroscopes controlled pitch and yaw and a barometric device monitored altitude. To measure distance to the target, a small propeller on the nose calculated the miles travelled. Once the desired range had been reached two detonators fired, causing the rudder and elevator to lock, sending the missile into a steep dive.

In May 1943 Hitler ordered a commission to determine whether the FZG 76 cruise missile or the Wehrmacht's A4 ballistic missile would be the preferred bombardment weapon. Both had advantages. The FZG 76 was inexpensive and simpler to operate, but it was vulnerable to interception. The A4, on the other hand, while being horribly expensive to manufacture and complicated to operate, was immune to interception. In the end the commission recommended that both be put into production. By the summer of 1943 the FZG 76 was at a point where plans for mass production could begin.

The V1 was one of the most distinctive flying machines to appear in the skies over Europe during World War II. From the outset it was to be produced as cheaply as possible, with the sole purpose of making a one-way flight lasting a maximum of 40 minutes. Because it was a pilotless aircraft it did not have to meet the high manufacturing tolerances needed for manned machines. Most of the aircraft was constructed from cheap mild steel, with a minimum of aerodynamic finesse. The Argus pulse-jet ran on low-grade (75-octane) fuel.

In April 1943 Oberst Max Wachtel was given command of the world's first cruise missile unit – *Lehr- und Erprobungskommando Wachtel* (Wachtel Training and Test

Outwardly, this Fi 103M-23 differs little from the final production Fi-103A-1. This missile was part of the *M-zellen* pre-production batch, and by September 1943 only 38 examples had been delivered. Fortunately for the Allies, the V1's guidance system was still not fully mature. If the attack on London had been launched in December 1943, fewer than one in six missiles would have reached Greater London. (National Museum of the United States Air Force)

Command). This unit was based at the Zempin test range near Peenemünde for training. By August only 60 per cent of the test launches had been successful. Not until September were 38 pre-production Fi 103s finally delivered to Wachtel's unit, with the first training launch taking place on 26 October.

Quantity production of the Fi 103 began in March 1944, although more testing was still required. Between 14 and 17 April the Luftwaffe launched 30 Fi 103s, nine of which crashed shortly after takeoff, with the remaining missiles striking within 30km (18 miles) of their target. Although the Fi 103 was never fully ready for combat operations, it was, nevertheless, a technical wonder. Not only was the Fi 103 the first jet-powered aircraft to enter operational service, it was also a completely new type of combat aircraft – a cruise missile.

All along the channel coast from Dieppe to Calais missile sites were being built and prepared for this new type of warfare. For the Luftwaffe, the Fi 103 simultaneously represented both a technical triumph and tactical failure. No longer able to field manned bombers, it now had to rely on a hastily manufactured pilotless aircraft to bomb a distant target. At approximately 0350 hrs on 13 June 1944 the world's first successful cruise missile attack began – nine V1s had been launched during the evening of 12 June, but none had reached England. What was to be a frightening roar turned into a muted bark. Of the ten missiles launched that morning six never made it across the channel. Of the four that did, the first crashed into the ground at Stone, near Dartford, two more came down on open land with no casualties, but the fourth found its mark, killing six people when it fell on Bethnal Green.

East
London

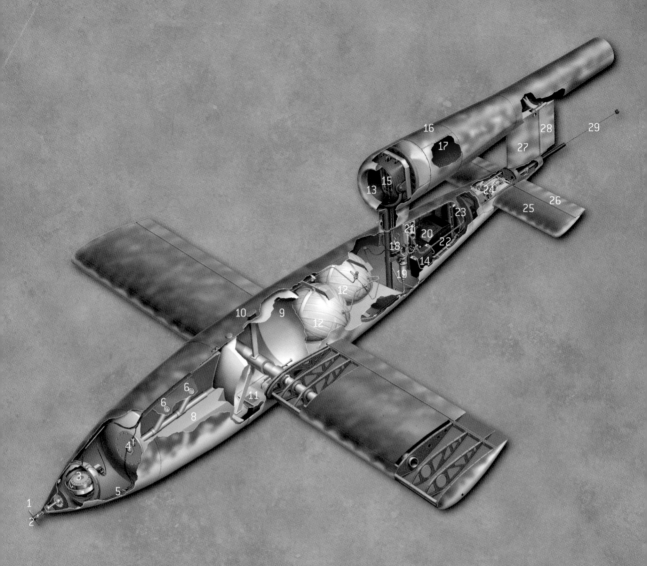

Fi 103A-1 CUTAWAY

1. Propeller for range control
2. Impact switch for fuses
3. Magnetic compass master gyro
4. Main fuse pocket
5. Belly landing fuse switch
6. Fuse pockets
7. Tubular wing spar
8. Fuel tank
9. Fuel tank
10. Lifting lug
11. Fuel tank filter
12. Wire-wound compressed air bottles
13. Air intake
14. Dry battery for electrical service
15. Flap valve grid and fuel jets

16. Spark plug
17. Combustion chamber
18. Fuel control mechanism
19. Fuel filter
20. Master gyro
21. Veeder counter
22. Altitude control
23. Secondary gyros
24. Pneumatic servo-motor operating rudder
25. Tailplane
26. Elevators
27. Vertical stabiliser
28. Rudder
29. FuG 23 radio antenna

TECHNICAL SPECIFICATIONS

METEOR

GLOSTER E.28/39 PIONEER

Britain's first jet aircraft was designed for the sole purpose of proving and testing Whittle's new turbojet engine. It was of all-metal, monocoque, construction, with the fuselage covered in a light alloy stressed skin. The Whittle W.1 engine was fitted in the rear fuselage and supported at four points on a tubular engine-bearing frame. At the maximum permitted 16,500rpm the W.1 developed a modest 860lb of thrust. An 81-gallon fuel tank was fitted between the engine and the cockpit, located forward. To ensure good takeoff characteristics, a tricycle undercarriage was fitted. W4041 first flew on 15 May 1941, followed by W4046 on 1 March 1943. The latter aircraft was powered by a new Rover W.2B engine, producing 1,200lb of thrust. W4046 would be lost on 30 July 1943 when Sqn Ldr Douglas Davie jammed the ailerons while in an inverted spin, forcing him to be the first pilot to bale out from a jet aircraft. W4041 would end its flying career in April 1944 after successfully completing its final ten-hour test programme. The two E.28/39s achieved a maximum speed of 466mph at 10,000ft.

As the sole surviving E.28/39, W4041 was earmarked for preservation immediately post-war, being put on permanent display in the Science Museum in Kensington on 29 April 1946 – a fitting resting place for such an historical aviation pioneer.

DG206/G was the first F.9/40 Meteor to take flight. Due to delays in the construction of W.2B engines by Rover, the Gloster test team was forced to equip DG206/G with Halford H.1 engines from de Havilland. The aircraft made its first flight, from RAF Cranwell, in Lincolnshire, on 5 March 1943 with test pilot Michael Daunt at the controls. This photograph was taken just a few days prior to its maiden flight. (Phil Jarrett)

F.9/40 METEOR

On 7 February 1941, MAP ordered 12 'Gloster Whittle aeroplanes' to specification F.9/40 under contract SB21179/C.23(a). The serial batch DG202–DG213 was allocated to the first 12 F.9/40s, but only eight prototypes were actually built. The construction of these aircraft followed accepted practices and used light aluminium alloys throughout. It was also a design that was short of any aerodynamic innovations. Gloster realised early on that an engine capable of developing 2,000lb of thrust would not be ready soon enough to develop the E.28/39 into a single-engined day fighter. George Carter, Gloster's chief designer, had no alternative but to select a twin-engined layout.

The over-riding demand in the specification called for a high-altitude fighter, fitted with a pressurised cockpit, that had a service ceiling of no less than 46,000ft. The all up weight of the F.9/40 was calculated at 11,755lb with a fuel load of 200 gallons, but no armament was installed. The highest speed obtained by an F.9/40 prototype was 488mph at 10,000ft.

The delayed delivery of the W.2B engine, built by the car manufacturer Rover, slowed the programme considerably. Indeed, it was not until 29 June 1942 that DG202/G began taxi trials with two 'ground only' engines. With no airworthy W.2Bs available by year end, Gloster decided to fit two Halford H.1 engines into DG206/G instead, and it duly made the Meteor's first flight on 5 March 1943. It was not until 24 July that DG202/G finally took to the air powered by W.2B engines. Ironically, the Americans, who had been supplied with drawings of Whittle's design in October 1941, flew the jet-powered Bell P-59A eight months *before* the W.2B engine was flown in the Meteor prototype! Frank Whittle said after the war:

> Both British Thompson-Houston and Rover attempted to improve on Power Jets design, and failed miserably. My Power Jets colleagues and I protested vigorously, only to make ourselves very unpopular. This very sorry state of affairs dragged on until early 1943 when, at last, Rolls-Royce took over from Rover. The scene changed overnight, Rolls-Royce getting the W.2B through the prescribed 125-hour type test, which saw the engine achieve its designed performance, within three months.
>
> In short, the succession of avoidable delays may have totalled about seven-and-a-half years. The RAF could have been equipped with Meteors and Vampires, or the like, by 1937.

Long before the first F.9/40 flew, the serious and somewhat confused business of naming the new fighter had begun. A lot of paper was passed between MAP and Gloster in the process. In August 1941, MAP informed the company that its favoured name of Avenger could not be used because it would be confused with the Vultee Vengeance dive-bomber! How the Grumman Avenger was missed is not known. MAP had settled on the name Thunderbolt, but had to be told by Gloster that this was taken by Republic Aviation's P-47. Finally, in February 1942, MAP chose the name Meteor, and it stuck.

METEOR G.41A Mk I

As construction of the F.9/40s neared completion, production arrangements for the operational G.41A Meteor Mk I forged ahead. On 12 January 1944 prototype EE210/G, flown by Michael Daunt, took to the air. Essentially, this was the military version of the F.9/40 powered by two Rolls-Royce W.2B/23C Welland Series 1 turbojets, each of which delivered 1,770lb of thrust.

Like the F.9/40 prototypes and the many other marks of Meteor that followed, the Mk I was of all-metal stressed skin construction. The fuselage was built around four light-alloy and steel longerons, with pressed light-alloy frames and rolled stringers. It was constructed in three separate sections – front fuselage, containing the nose landing gear, cockpit, armament and ammunition bay; centre section, carrying the main fuel tank and provision for a ventral tank, main landing gear, engines, flaps and air brakes; and rear fuselage and lower fin. The wing was constructed around two light-alloy and steel spars, with main ribs at the root, inboard and outboard of the engines. The tail section was a one-piece unit with elevators, top fin and top and bottom rudder. Flight controls consisted of push rods and cables to the tail unit and push rods to the ailerons.

The fighter's armament comprised four short-barrel Hispano Mk III 20mm cannons, with 780 rounds in total for 16 seconds of firing. Early in the war it had been found that solid ball projectiles were just a destructive as high explosive rounds (HE),

Meteor EE210/G was the first Mk I off the production line. In exchange for Bell Airacomet YP-59A RJ362/G, EE210/G was shipped to Muroc Field, California. Here, marked with 'stars and bars', it was flown for the first time by John Grierson on 15 April 1944. By December the aircraft had been shipped back to the UK and the RAE, and it was subsequently transferred to Maintenance Command in March 1946 and given the ground instructional serial 5873M. (National Museum of the United States Air Force)

What the Meteor I lacked in overall performance when compared with its piston-engined single-seat contemporaries, it more than made up for it when it came to armament. The 20mm Hispano Mk III cannon was arguably the finest air-to-air weapon built by the Allies in World War II. The Mk III was shorter, lighter and had a higher rate of fire when compared with the Mk II cannon fitted in the Tempest V. (Author's Collection)

so a 50:50 mix of HE/incendiary and semi-armour-piercing incendiary rounds was quickly adopted. Outwardly, the Mk I differed little from the original prototypes. There were some airframe refinements, including a clear-view transparent canopy, along with the fitment of five-degree dihedral wing tips.

In terms of performance the new Meteor I was disappointing. Although faster than the leading piston-engined fighters of the day, it suffered from limited range (endurance of 40–45 minutes) and a poor rate of climb. The jet's shortcomings were revealed in a report written in September 1944 by the commanding officer of No. 616 Sqn, Wg Cdr Andrew McDowall:

It will be seen that the Meteor Mk I at present suffers from various technical limitations which considerably restrict its use operationally. The following figures of speed and rate of climb of Meteor I and other types are interesting.

At 10,000ft	Meteor I	Spitfire XIV	Mustang III	Tempest V
Rate of climb in feet per minute	2,300	4,400	3,600	2,900

METEOR CANNONS

Equipped with four Hispano Mk III 20mm cannons, the Meteor I was arguably the best-armed day fighter assigned to ADGB during the anti-Diver campaign. These weapons had a rate-of-fire of 750 rounds per minute and each gun had a magazine that could hold 195 rounds, giving the pilot 16 seconds of firing time. A 50:50 mix of HE/incendiary and semi-armour-piercing incendiary rounds was typically loaded into the fighter's magazines.

Speed (mph)	430	403	403	402
At 15,000ft	Meteor I	Spitfire XIV	Mustang III	Tempest V
Rate of climb in				
feet per minute	2,250	3,700	3,000	2,730
Speed (mph)	436	415	425	411

From these figures it will be seen that while the Meteor I is faster than the other types, it is considerably inferior in rate of climb.

Twenty Meteor Is were ordered and 16 would serve with No. 616 Sqn, the first of these being delivered to the unit at Farnborough in July 1944. Conversion to the new fighter, however, had begun three months earlier when EE213/G and EE214/G (then in non-combat condition) were used as trainers, again at Farnborough, and were later brought up to operational standards and flown to the unit's new frontline base at Manston, Kent, on 21 July. Among the first to convert to the Meteor in April was Sqn Ldr Dennis Barry, one of No. 616 Sqn's flight commanders:

There were no Pilot's Notes available, but we felt confident, if a little over-awed at the prospect of being chosen to fly such a novel aircraft and the honour accorded to 616. As I taxied out to the end of the Farnborough runway in Meteor Mk I EE214/G [later coded YQ-B], I ran through the drill as briefed and I then positioned the aircraft ready for takeoff. Throttles forward, maximum power while holding on the brakes, then brakes released and slowly accelerate down the runway. No swing, no drag, and hold the stick level until 80mph indicated, then ease the stick back and lift off the runway at 120mph. The rate of climb was initially poor at 500ft per minute, but as the power built up the rate increased.

Local flying now, the aircraft was quiet with no noise from the engines, only a 'whooshing' sound from the air passing the cockpit, like a glider. The visibility was good, with only a shallow nose in front, and was similar to being in an airship's observation car. The Meteor felt heavy on the controls compared with the Spitfire, especially when full of fuel. After a 40-minute flight it was time to land, remembering that by 600ft we had to decide whether to land or to carry on ahead because of the limited power available for an overshoot once we were below the decision height. Landing successfully completed, I returned to my colleagues satisfied with the aircraft, except for the lack of power.

Test pilot Capt Eric Brown was the first naval aviator to fly a jet aircraft, taking Meteor I EE214/G aloft in early 1944. His thoughts were not flattering:

Exciting as that event was for me, it could not conceal the fact that the Meteor I was a rather mediocre aeroplane from the handling

An unidentified No. 616 Sqn pilot is strapped in prior to another anti-Diver patrol. Meteor pilots found the aircraft 'pleasant to fly at low level', with a good all-round view. While the view from the heavily framed cockpit was good, pilots found the visibility to the sides and rear of the cockpit to be poor. Pilot protection consisted of a sheet of armour plate 7mm thick located behind the pilot. The sideways-opening canopy was replaced by a sliding hood from the Meteor III onwards, whilst the Mk I's distinctive upright windscreen was made more streamlined. (Author's Collection)

standpoint. Besides being underpowered, it had heavy ailerons, suffered from directional instability and had terrible forward view in rain.

As previously noted, No. 616 Sqn would receive 16 Meteor Is in total, comprising serials EE213 to EE222 and EE224 to EE229. Meteors EE210, EE211 and EE212 went to the Royal Aircraft Establishment and EE223 was used for engine development by Rolls-Royce.

METEOR Mk II

Delivery delays of the Rover W.2B engines for the F.9/40 prototype prompted MAP to instruct Gloster to give priority to a Halford H.1-powered prototype designated the Meteor II (Airframe DG207/G). Due to the priority given to the Halford Goblin-powered de Havilland Vampire, production of the Meteor II did not go beyond this one prototype.

METEOR Mk III

The Meteor III did not see action against the V1 flying bomb. Designed to take advantage of the more powerful Rolls-Royce W.2B/37 Derwent I engine (2,000lb of thrust), the Mk III incorporated a sliding canopy with better all-round vision, increased fuel capacity, slotted air brakes and a strengthened airframe. The first 15 Mk IIIs delivered, however, were powered by W.2B/23C Wellands as fitted in the Mk I, No. 616 Sqn having to wait until December 1944 to receive its first Derwent-powered Meteor III. The new engines gave the fighter an improved top speed of 465mph at sea level and 485mph at 30,000ft. On 4 February 1945 No. 616 Sqn sent four Mk IIIs to Melsbroek airfield in Belgium. By 30 March 17 Meteor IIIs were on the continent, but no aerial claims were made by the unit prior to VE-Day.

Having its spine-mounted fuel tank replenished, Meteor I EE219 heads a line up of Meteor IIIs at Manston in late January 1945. Note the Spitfire IXs parked behind the jets. EE219 later spent time with the RAE before being sent to Maintenance Command in January 1946 and given ground instructional serial 5799M. (Graham Pitchfork)

Gloster Meteor I	
Dimensions	
Wingspan	43ft 0in
Length	41ft 3in
Height	13ft 0in
Wing area	374 sq. ft
Armament	4 x Hispano Mk III 20mm cannons
Weight (lb)	
Empty	8,140
Loaded	13,795
Performance	
Engines	Two 1,700lb thrust Rolls-Royce W.2B/23C Welland Series I turbojets
Maximum speed	415mph at 10,000ft
Range	580 miles
Climb to	30,000ft 15 minutes
Useful Ceiling	40,000ft

V1 FLYING BOMB

FIESELER Fi 103

Revolutionary in concept and design, the Fi 103 was in many ways the 'Sten gun' of the air – the Sten gun was a cheap mass-produced British sub-machine gun made from stamped metal parts. As one of the world's first jet-powered aircraft to enter combat and the world's first cruise missile, the Fi 103 was a remarkable feat of engineering, but it was also rather crude and cheap in many respects. Simplicity was the watchword for the Fi 103. Made almost entirely of welded mild-steel plate and wood, it was powered by the most straightforward of jet engines – the pulse-jet. And as a one-shot disposable weapon, it did not need the same aerodynamic refinements that were required for a manned aircraft, or the skilled labour to build it.

The heart of the Fi 103 centred around the fuel tank, which was the backbone of the whole structure. A plain cylinder with domed ends, the tank carried the bottom launching rail and the top lifting lug. It was this structure that had to absorb the violent catapulting forces, which could be as high as 10g. The fuel was also high-pressured, measuring 100lb per square inch. In order to deal with these stresses the main tank was built of heavy, 12-gauge mild-steel plate.

Directly in front of the fuel tank sat the warhead. Weighing in at 850kg (1,870lb), it was attached by four bolts with external lugs. The warhead casing itself was only

A British soldier examines two wire bound compressed air bottles found at a wrecked V1 site in northern France. These two spheres contained the compressed air necessary to power the V1's gyroscopes, force fuel into the pulse-jet engine and operate the pneumatic servos that controlled the rudder and elevators. (NARA)

2mm (0.078in) thick. This gave it the maximum weight of explosive in order to create the biggest blast, the warhead being fitted with two Z80A impact fuses. At the very front of the Fi 103 was the detachable nose cone, which housed the compass and air pilot propeller. To keep magnetic interference to a minimum, the nose cone was made of a duralumin alloy, while the compass sat in a large bowl-shaped wooden receptacle.

If the fuel tank was the heart of the Fi 103, then the compressed air bottles were the muscle. Located directly behind the fuel tank, they were slightly staggered to the left and right of the fuselage axis. Wire bound on the outside (using 16-gauge piano wire), with a welded mild-steel construction on the inside, these spheres contained the compressed air vital for Fi 103 flight operations. The contents of the air bottles was used threefold – to keep the gyros spinning, forcing fuel to the Argus motor and operating the pneumatic servos in the rudder and elevators.

The V1's wings, fitted before launch, consisted of sheets of mild steel spot-welded to the internal ribs. This made for an extremely strong structure, which was perfectly flush with no protruding rivet heads.

Powering the V1 was the Argus 109-014 pulse-jet engine. Made from a sheet of mild steel rolled into a tube, it was a model of simplicity and low cost. At the heart of the engine was the engine shutter assembly. This consisted of a matrix of vanes and fuel injectors located at the front of the engine. Able to use any grade of petroleum, the Argus engine was designed for a one-way flight, and had an operational life of approximately one hour. Once the engine had been started, each pulse or cycle of the engine began with the shutters open. Fuel was then injected behind them and ignited, the resulting explosion forced the shutters closed. Following the explosion, the pressure in the engine dropped, causing the shutters to reopen – the cycle was repeated roughly 45 to 55 times per second. Fuel burn was about 4.54 litres (1 gallon) every ten seconds, which translated into 1.6km (1 mile) of distance. The V1 had many names, but two of them, 'buzzbomb' and 'doodlebug', were derived from the sputtering sound the pulse-jet made while in flight.

The V1's Askania automatic pilot consisted of three air-driven gyros (a master and two secondary gyros). The master gyro controlled both elevators and rudder, while the secondary devices provided damping against oscillations. In order to counter the main gyro's tendency to wander off its initial setting, the magnetic compass was directly connected to it, providing corrections in the horizontal plane during flight.

One of the most important pieces of equipment fitted to the V1 was the air pilot propeller or air log veeder-type mechanical counter. Responsible for arming the warhead after some 60km (37 miles) of flight, it also controlled the V1's range. Before launch the veeder counter would be set with a pre-determined figure. During flight the propeller would spin and the counter would return gradually to zero. Once that figure was reached, explosive bolts would be fired, forcing the small elevators on the tailplane into the down position and locking the rudder. Pushed into a steep dive, the V1 would then plunge towards its target. The Germans predicted that 90 per cent of the V1s would hit within a circle 10km (6 miles) around a target, and the rest would land within 6km (3.7 miles).

The early Fi 103s were categorised in three batches – the *V-zellen* (*Vorsienzellen*, prototype airframes), *M-zellen* (*Modellserienzellen*, pre-production) and *G-zellen*

V1 WARHEAD

The warhead installed in the Fi 103 consisted of 850kg (1,870lb) of Amatol high explosive fitted with a Z80A mechanical all-ways impact fuse, an El.A.Z 106 electrical impact fuse and a 17B mechanical clockwork delayed-action fuse. The fusing was very reliable, and very few V1s failed to detonate upon hitting the ground. The warhead, cased in sheet steel 1.27mm (0.05in) thick, was bolted to the forward end of the fuel tank. Ahead of this was a light-alloy nose that housed the magnetic compass master gyro and the fuse pressure plate. Note also the windmill propeller for range control.

The Askania Werke AG automatic pilot control unit was critical component for the Fi 103. The autopilot was comprised of height and range setters, one gyro control for pitch and yaw and two gyro controls for rate of climb and turn. (National Museum of the United States Air Force)

Automatic Pilot Control Unit V-1

(*Grosserienzellen*, serial production). Some 200 *V-zellen* airframes had been planned, but only 120 were actually completed and most had been launched by the summer of 1943. By September of that year just 38 *M-zellen* missiles had been delivered, with the first test launch not occurring until 26 October.

When the Fi 103 finally commenced quantity production in March 1944, the time it took to manufacture the missile had been reduced to just 350 hours – 120 of which were reserved for constructing the complicated autopilot.

Fi 103A-1

Well before the world's first cruise missile attack was launched, the defects of the Fi 103 were well known, but repeated requests for changes were ignored. As a result, all of the missiles launched in the summer of 1944 were the basic Fi 103A-1 model. It was powered by the Argus 109-014 pulse-jet engine and carried 610 litres (133 gallons) of fuel, which gave the weapon a range of 200–210km (125–130 miles). Top speed was 670kmh at 1,375m (415mph at 4,500ft), and it carried a warhead made up of 850kg (1,870lb) of Amatol 39A high explosive. To enhance the explosive effect of the Fi 103 Hitler ordered that 250 V1 warheads per month be filled with Trialen. The first of these were used on 18 July 1944.

Fi 103B-1

This was the wooden-winged version of the Fi 103A-1. The wings had a slightly larger span, and reduced the wing weight by 38kg (85lb). Plywood was also substituted in some of the nose construction. It was first launched in February 1945.

Fi 103B-2

Similar to the B-1, the B-2 had a Trialen-packed explosive warhead and improved fusing. Missiles with Trialen-equipped warheads sometimes had a large red X painted on either side of the warhead casing.

Fi 103C-1

The C-1 used a lighter SC 800 aircraft fragmentation bomb to give the weapon an extended range.

Fi 103D-1

The D-1 was designed to carry a chemical warhead, but this version did not go into series production.

Fi 103E-1

The E-1 was designed for launch from sites in Holland. It was fitted with wooden wings, an enlarged fuel tank of 810 litres (178 gallons) and a smaller plywood-encased warhead.

Fi 103F-1

The F-1 was the definitive long-range version, with a fuel load of 1,025 litres (225 gallons) and a reduced warhead of 530kg (1,168lb). The missile was powered by an Argus 109-44 engine.

The V1 had many and varied codenames, with manufacturer Fieseler designating it the Fi 103 and the Luftwaffe using FZG 76 and *Kirschkern* (Cherry Stone). On 30 April 1944 Hitler ordered that FZG 76 and *Kirschkern* be replaced by *Maikafer* (June Bug). German propaganda started using the term V1 in June 1944, and Hitler again changed the codename to *Krahe* (Crow) five months later. Here, one of the *V-zellen* (prototypes) is readied for launch at the test range near Peenemünde in the spring of 1943. (Author's Collection)

Fi 103A-1	
Dimensions	
Wingspan	5.33m (17ft 6in)
Fuselage length	6.65m (21ft 10in)
Overall length	7.73m (25ft 4in)
Fuselage diameter	0.825m (2ft 8in)
Armament	850kg (1,870lb) Amatol high explosive warhead, fitted with redundant impact fuses
Guidance	Askania pre-set autopilot with gyro inertial platform and magnetic compass
Weights	
Launch weight	2,200kg (4,858lb)
Fuel	610 litres (133 gallons) E-1 aviation gasoline
Performance	
Engine	Argus 109-014 pulse-jet
Maximum thrust	310kg (683lb) at 1,000m (3,280ft) at 700kmh (434mph)
Maximum cruise speed	670kmh (415mph) at 1,375m (4,500ft)
Maximum range	200–210km (125–130 miles)
Theoretical rate of fire	72 per launcher per day
Maximum actual rate	Three per day in 1944
Accuracy (ground-launched)	Circular error probability of 13km (8 miles)

THE STRATEGIC
SITUATION

It had been a devastating attack. For seven hours more than 300 Luftwaffe bombers hammered London with a mix of high explosive and incendiary bombs. The night of 10/11 May 1941 was the Luftwaffe's last large-scale attempt to bomb Britain into submission. The Battle of Britain and the night Blitz that followed had shown that Germany could be defeated. The Luftwaffe's aim of destroying British morale by targeting its largest cities and civilian population had failed miserably. Not only had it stiffened British resolve, it gave them the determination to pursue an area-bombing campaign of their own.

While the RAF's early results were disappointing (the number of bombers dispatched on any given night ranged from 80 to just over 100), Bomber Command steadily grew in strength and experience. On the night of 28/29 March 1942, Bomber Command had its first major success. With the help of an almost full moon, 234 aircraft – 146 Wellingtons, 41 Hampdens, 26 Stirlings and 21 Manchesters – approached the historic German city of Lübeck. The defences were light, giving crews the option of attacking from low level. More than 400 tons of bombs were dropped, two-thirds being incendiary. The aiming point was the centre of town – built of narrow streets and old, half-timbered buildings.

As a pure area-bombing fire raid it was an example of what could be accomplished when the conditions were right. Nearly 30 per cent of Lübeck's built-up area had been destroyed by fire. The casualties numbered between 312 and 320 killed, making it the heaviest death toll in a German raid up to that point in the war. Hitler was enraged, and demanded retaliatory strikes against Britain. This in turn lead to the Baedeker

Blitz, named after the famous 19th-century German tourist guidebooks, which listed Britain's centres of cultural interest. These raids, which lasted until January 1943, achieved relatively little owing to the lack of available aircraft and trained crews to man them. It was a campaign of no military value.

By March 1942 both the Wehrmacht and the Luftwaffe were fully committed to the battle raging deep inside the Soviet Union and the precarious situation in North Africa. The Luftwaffe units that remained in the west were mainly equipped with single-seat Bf 109Fs and Fw 190As. The best they could do was to launch fighter-bomber attacks against targets in England. These 'tip and run' raids began in March 1942 and ended in June 1943. Targeting Allied shipping and coastal military and industrial installations on the southern coast of England, these attacks were in fact the most effective launched by the Luftwaffe on this front during the entire war. In some cases they were 100 per cent effective.

These bombing raids were carried out at very low level and at great speed. Armed with a single 250 or 500kg bomb, Bf 109s and Fw 190s would attack singly or in formation. For the British, there was no effective way to defend against these raids. Unable to detect the fighter-bombers by radar owing to their wave-skimming approach heights, RAF fighters could only react after the fact. It was a frustrating and embarrassing affair.

One of the most effective raids occurred on 20 January 1943 when a force of 25 Fw 190A-4 fighter-bombers from 10(*Jabo*)./JG 26 successfully bombed south London. With impunity, the fighter-bombers dropped their bombs and strafed buildings and targets of opportunity. The results were shocking – 38 children and six teachers were killed, along with 26 other civilians. It was a serious setback for the British, and one that resulted in the problem of *Jabo* attacks being debated in the House of Commons for the first time. While the Secretary of State assured the public that everything was being done to combat the raids, the fact remained that Britain's capital city had been bombed in broad daylight by a force that had penetrated nearly 100 miles at high speed, dropped its bombs and escaped virtually unscathed. Intercepted by RAF Spitfires and Typhoons as they crossed the coast for France near Dover, the Luftwaffe lost four Bf 109G-4s and three Fw 190A-4s out of a force of 112 aircraft committed that day. It was a foreshadowing of things to come.

A rather casual scene as V1 launch technicians discuss their next move during testing of an early prototype missile at Peenemünde in the autumn of 1943. The early, unsuccessful, Rheinmetal Borsig launcher seen here was replaced by the Walter WR 2.3 *Schlitzrohrschleuder*. (Author's Collection)

A month earlier, on 24 December 1942, the first powered launch and flight of a V1 had taken place at Peenemünde. While this event represented a key step forward in the V-weapon programme, December 1942 would also prove to be a major turning point for the Wehrmacht. In North Africa, Rommel and the *Deutsches Afrikakorps* had commenced their long last stand in Tunisia, whilst at Stalingrad the German Sixth Army was completely surrounded, facing certain annihilation. On 2 February 1943, unable to fight its way out, the Sixth Army surrendered, ending the battle of Stalingrad. It was a crushing defeat, and for the first time during the war the German public was informed. The Third Reich's power and dominance had reached its peak. The great victories attained in the first two-and-a-half years of the war were over. Germany would now fight a long and bitter defensive struggle, with Hitler demanding more from his armed forces fuelled by an irrational demand for vengeance.

Hitler's hope for retribution lay with the new V1 and V2 missiles. Well before the first V1 was successfully launched, British Intelligence was aware of the German long-range rocket programme, and its potential consequences. In fact the V1 was not discovered until after the existence of the potentially deadly V2 had been proven. On 25 September 1943 Dr R. V. Jones of Air Ministry Scientific Intelligence warned in a report that 'it is possible that the German Air Force has also been developing a pilotless aircraft for long-range bombardment in competition with the Army rocket'.

Indeed, by November, new evidence began to surface. A French agent reported the locations of six 'secret weapon sites' near Abbeville. Up to that point the Allies had very little information regarding the V1. Apart from some photo-reconnaissance images that showed 'a small pilotless aircraft sitting on the end of a firing ramp' and the German code name 'FZG 76', which stood for *Flakzielgerät* (anti-aircraft target device), they were in the dark. This new threat was, however, taken seriously by the Chiefs of Staff, the end result being the instigation of Operation *Crossbow* (the destruction of missile and storage sites in France). By December 1943 more than half of the V1 sites in northern France were complete, and by late January the Allies had identified all 96 of them.

Crossbow had commenced on 5 December, with the targeting of V1 sites being shared between RAF Bomber Command, the USAAF's Eighth and Ninth Air Forces and the 2nd Tactical Air Force (TAF). The campaign, while costly in terms of the number of aircraft and crews lost (the majority to flak), pulverised most, if not all, of the permanent sites, and it was believed at the time to have delayed the start of the missile attacks on London by a full six months. *Crossbow* forced the Germans to build 'modified sites' that were easier to construct and more difficult to locate and destroy. Indeed the *Flak-Regiment* 155(W) war diary reported that none of the new sites had been located by the Allies come June 1944.

Operation *Crossbow* was the codename given by the Allies to the aerial assault on all V1 launch sites and storage areas. The attacks began on 5 December 1943, with the RAF and the USAAF using everything at their disposal, including heavy and medium bombers and fighter-bombers. This Ninth Air Force aerial reconnaissance photograph clearly shows that these relentless attacks had systematically destroyed the large concrete permanent Site System 1 in the Pas-de-Calais. Its associated storage sheds (S-1, S-2 and S-3), assembly buildings (Q, R-1 and R-2) and the launching platform (P) have also been damaged. (NARA)

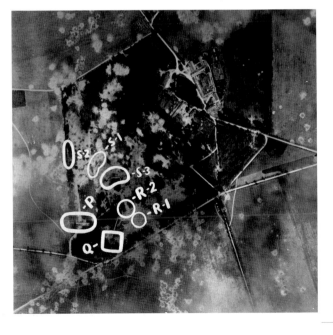

The last line of defence. When a V1 made it through the anti-aircraft gun belt and fighter patrols, the only thing left in its path was a huge balloon barrage south of London. This 'pneumatic forest' was a passive defensive system that, by 15 July 1944, consisted of 1,247 balloons. When a V1 hit one of the suspended cables the results were often fatal – the cable wrapped around this missile's wing caused it to crash. The balloon barrage was credited with bringing down 231 V1s. (NARA)

The real delay in getting the V1 into service was caused by the strategic bombing of German aircraft factories, which resulted in the mass production of Fi 103s slipping from the autumn of 1943 to the spring of 1944.

While the Allies were bombing V1 sites and storage areas, the Germans were determined to 'avenge the terror attacks by the enemy' with Operation *Steinbock* – a renewed bombing campaign against London that began during the evening of 21 January 1944. On the night of 18/19 April London was subject to its last major bombing raid of the war. Of the 125 aircraft sent to attack the capital, only half managed to hit their target, for the loss of 13 bombers. These raids were for propaganda purposes only, with the Germans claiming that 600 bombers had attacked London, with devastating results.

In parallel with Operation *Crossbow*, the plan to defend Britain against V1 attack was codenamed *Diver*. It fell to Air Marshal Sir Roderic Hill, head of ADGB, and Maj Gen Sir Frederick Pile of AA Command to devise an effective defence of southeast England. Believing the Germans would be able to launch two V1s per hour from existing sites towards London, they devised a defensive plan that incorporated a mix of heavy and light anti-aircraft guns, search lights, barrage balloons and both day and nightfighters.

Through five years of war the Germans had tried to bomb the British in submission. They had used everything at their disposal, including heavy and medium bombers, dive-bombers and fighter-bombers. From the Pas-de-Calais, large railway guns and coastal batteries had lobbed shells at southern England, and naval vessels had also targeted coastal towns and installations with gunfire. It was, in the end, a campaign of half attempts that was ultimately doomed to failure because of a dysfunctional command structure. With no clear military objective in mind, the Germans squandered their limited forces. Fortunately for the Allies, the Luftwaffe was unaware of how successful its 'tip and run' raids had really been in 1942–43. Now, in the summer of 1944, the Germans had a new weapon – one that could be used both day and night, in all weather.

On 8 June, two days after the successful invasion of Normandy, Maj Gen Pile received word from Chiefs of Staff that the flying bomb threat had 'entirely disappeared' and Operation *Diver* would not take place. At 0418 hrs on Tuesday, 13 June 1944, the first flying bomb to strike Britain during World War II came crashing to earth at Swanscombe, near Dartford. Exploding harmlessly on agricultural land bordering the A2 Rochester–Dartford road, it was followed by three more, which struck sequentially in Cuckfield, Sussex, at Bethnal Green in London and at Platt, near Sevenoaks in Kent. The Chiefs of Staff believed that these missiles 'were only test firings', but between the evening of 15 June and midday on the 16th, 244 V1s were launched towards the capital, with 73 reaching Greater London and a further 50 or so landing around Southampton. The 'testing' was over and the battle had begun. It would be a long campaign, with the last V1s to reach Britain arriving on 29 March 1945.

THE COMBATANTS

RAF PILOT TRAINING

On 5 June 1944, the greatest seaborne invasion in history was just hours away. Across England a vast Allied air armada was poised to strike. As pilots and aircrew readied their machines, they had the confidence of knowing that their training, leadership and equipment was the best in the world. They would also be present over the invasion beaches in record numbers. The RAF would commit no fewer than 254 squadrons (a mix of British, Canadian, Polish, Czech, Dutch, Norwegian, French, Belgian, Australian and New Zealand units) of fighters, fighter-bombers, nightfighters, reconnaissance, medium and heavy bombers, to the Normandy invasion. The American contribution was even greater, totalling 376 squadrons. It could be well argued that the RAF and USAAF in 1944–45 were the best-trained and equipped air arms the world has ever seen.

In sharp contrast, the opposing Luftwaffe forces in Normandy numbered in the hundreds (500 serviceable aircraft, of which 160 were day fighters). These units would have no impact on the battle itself. In comparison to the Allies, whose forces had swelled to great numbers in the run up to D-Day, the Luftwaffe in France was a spent force. Indeed, only its flak arm and nightfighter force remained effective.

By 1944 RAF fighter pilots possessed an advantage of considerable value over many of their German counterparts. As graduates of the very successful British Commonwealth Air Training Plan (BCATP), they benefited from many years of air fighting where their losses had been low. As a consequence relatively few pilots in

Fighter Command units were new or inexperienced. Many had flown on operations for lengthy periods, with a high number of squadron and flight commanders on their second or third tours. In addition, a large contingent of RCAF home defence pilots and instructors had now been redeployed to the UK. Although combat neophytes, they were all highly experienced flyers.

By 1944 the vast majority of pilots who served in the RAF had been trained through the BCATP or had been exposed to the American system. Set up after the outbreak of war, Canada was given the task of aircrew training, which in turn gave birth to the BCATP. Flying schools in South Africa, Rhodesia and Australia soon followed.

The BCATP syllabus began with the aircrew selection board. There, the young volunteer would face two or three officers, and within minutes his fate was decided. There were no second chances, and if he failed to impress the board his feet would remain firmly on the ground. For the successful candidate, the assembly-line process of aircrew training would begin. The manning depot was the next stop for a new trainee, where he once again faced a succession of interviews, lectures, tests and countless hours of drill. He also spent one or two hours in the Link trainer, the 1940s version of today's flight simulator. If the aspiring pilot found the process a difficult one to master he soon found himself being asked to choose another aircrew vocation.

Those who survived the manning depot were posted to an Elementary Flying Training School (EFTS), where they were sent aloft in two-seat de Havilland Tiger Moths, Fleet Finchs or Miles Magister – all fabric-covered open cockpit basic trainers.

It was at EFTS that the young student pilot, for the first time, came face to face with the mystical forces of flight. Being able to master the control column and rudder in order to keep the aircraft heading straight was a major first step. The student would also face a barrage of information about drag and lift, longitudinal stability, angle of incidence, stalling, spinning and side-slipping. On the ground, why these phenomenon occurred, and the correct way to deal with them, all made sense, but once in the air the chalkboard words were quickly blown away. On average, one in four students washed out during elementary training.

After three months of flying, and logging approximately 78 hours, the new cadet was then posted to a Service Flying Training School (SFTS) equipped with bigger, more powerful aircraft. Those selected for multi-engined machines moved on to Ansons, Oxfords or Cranes, whilst pilots headed for fighters were introduced to the North American Harvard. With a fully enclosed cockpit, the Harvard was a sea of instruments powered by a big Pratt & Whitney radial engine, and at low speeds it sometimes dropped a wing and snapped into a spin. If you could handle the Harvard you were then judged able to fly a frontline fighter. To reach that point the student had to complete a further 120 hours (including 20 hours of night flying) during three-and-a-half months of flying. Finally, with 200 hours in his logbook, the cadet was awarded his wings.

Upon their arrival in England, these newly minted pilots were assigned to an Advanced Flying Unit and trained to fly in British weather and black out conditions. When flying in North America, southern Africa or Australia, few student pilots had experienced the mist, rain and poor visibility that routinely blighted Britain. Having survived this, the pilot's second to last step before being assigned to a frontline

A graduate of the BCTAP, followed by numerous operational sorties in the Spitfire, Flg Off 'Dixie' Dean found conversion to the Meteor I a straightforward task during the spring of 1944. Having achieved the unit's first success against the V1, he would finish the anti-Diver campaign as No. 616 Sqn's most successful pilot, with three missiles to his credit. Having tipped the first one over with his wingtip, Dean shot the other two down with the jet's 20mm cannons. He is seen here with a Meteor III in Germany in the late spring of 1945. (Graham Pitchfork)

squadron was the Operational Training Unit (OTU). By 1943 there were eight OTUs dedicated to the training of single-engined fighter pilots. Many of the OTU aircraft were 'de-rated', meaning that they were no longer fit for combat duty and well past their prime. Here, the young aviators would learn to fly the aircraft they would use on operations.

By 1944 RAF fighter pilots would enter squadron service with a minimum of 270 hours of flight time. They also benefited from enhanced tactics and weapons training in the form of Combat Training Wings. Wing leaders, squadron commanders or junior officers with potential were also nurtured during a posting to the Fighter Leaders' School.

For the pilots of No. 616 Sqn in the summer of 1944, experience was not an issue. For 18 months prior to D-Day, they had flown countless bomber escort and fighter sweep missions in preparation for the invasion. There was not much they had not seen over France, and they were well versed in radar control and the procedures required to defend southern England against the fast, low-flying V1 menace.

In April 1944 the CO of the unit, Sqn Ldr Leslie Watts, was informed of the decision that No. 616 Sqn was to re-equip with a 'secret aircraft'. Although not officially recorded, it is almost certain that the unit had been chosen to be 'first in jet fighters' by one of its founder members, South Yorkshireman, ex-Battle of Britain pilot and Spitfire ace Sqn Ldr Ken Holden. He was on the staff of the Plans Division at Headquarters Fighter Command just as the Meteor I was nearing frontline readiness.

Conversion to the new fighter was straightforward and not unusual for the day, as Flg Off Mike Cooper recalled:

Meteor I EE213 or EE214 (note the Trainer Yellow undersides) is stripped down for maintenance at Manston, exposing one of its Rolls-Royce W.2B/23C Welland engines. In the background, the Meteor's fuel tank has also been uncovered on the spine of the jet. Like all British single-seat fighters, the Meteor I suffered from short range and endurance. Its total fuel load was just 300 gallons, giving the aircraft approximately 45 minutes of flight time. The fighter used Kerosene A.V./Turbine Ref. No. 34A/179, into which 1 per cent of lubricating oil had been mixed. (Author's Collection)

Sqn Ldr Watts and I were introduced to Wg Cdr Willie Wilson, CO of the experimental flight at Farnborough, at his caravan [on 27 May 1944]. He was most pleasant and easy going. He handed each of us a sheet of paper on which was typed 'pilot's notes', which explained how to start up and fly the aircraft. We were each led to an aircraft and climbed into the cockpit and studied the notes. After completing the study we reported back to the Wing Commander, who asked us if there were any problems? We both said no, to which he replied 'then fly the bloody things'.

The CO took EE214 and I flew EE213, and we experienced very little trouble. We each had two flights that day, and a further two the following day. We believed we were the first two squadron pilots, as opposed to test pilots, to fly the Meteor.

No. 616 Sqn's two-letter code 'YQ' is carefully applied to an unidentified Meteor I, probably at Manston. All Mk Is were camouflaged in Dark Green and Ocean Grey (the true factory-applied MAP shade, and not the mixed shade of Medium Sea Grey and Night used in the field). The uppersurface camouflage was based on MAP's pattern No. 2, which gave the recommended areas of Dark Green and Ocean Grey for monoplanes with a wingspan of under 70ft. (Author's Collection)

METEOR I COCKPIT

1. Gunsight
2. Cockpit lights (x 2)
3. Compass indicator
4. Airspeed indicator
5. Artificial horizon
6. Rate-of-climb indicator
7. Hood jettison handle
8. Clock
9. Main fuel tank gauges (x 2)
10. Turn-and-slip indicator
11. Direction indicator
12. Altimeter
13. Flap position indicator
14. Undercarriage indicator
15. Undercarriage control lever
16. Rudder pedals adjuster release
17. Engine RPM indicators (x 2)
18. Jet exhaust temperature gauge
19. Oxygen controls
20. IFF demolition switches
21. Burner pressure gauges (x 2)
22. Oil pressure gauge and temperature gauges (x 2)
23. Relighting switches
24. Landing lamp switch
25. Engine starter push buttons (x 2)
26. Air brakes control
27. Ammunition rounds counter
28. Throttle control lever
29. Radio control panel
30. Low oil pressure pump switches
31. Low oil pressure pump test buttons
32. Elevator trim wheel
33. Trim indicators
34. Rudder trim control
35. 'G' switches
36. Fuel balance cock control
37. Rudder pedals (x 2)
38. Control column
39. Gun firing button
40. Seat adjusting lever
41. Hydraulic emergency hand pump
42. Windscreen deicing pump
43. Engine high and low pressure cock controls
44. Emergency light switch
45. Harness release lever
46. Hood winding handle
47. Gyro gunsight dimmer control
48. Identification light selector switch
49. Camera master, navigation lights, pressure head heater, landing lights and RI compass switches
50. Pilot's seat

Two Hispano Mk III 20mm cannons are installed and checked by No. 616 Sqn armourers. A Mk III cannon, which weighed 84lb when installed, could fire 750 rounds per minute. (Author's Collection)

The rest of the squadron's pilots would have the unpleasant experience of flying a twin-engined Oxford to practise asymmetric flying before getting their hands on the Meteor.

As the D-Day battle unfolded No. 616 Sqn continued to fly their Spitfire VIIs in support of the invasion, undertaking beachhead patrols. At the same time, pilots were withdrawn from operations in groups of five at a time to begin conversion to the new fighter, which was initially carried out at Farnborough. Sqn Ldr Dennis Barry recalled the excitement surrounding the unit's re-equipment with the new fighter:

> The news that No. 616 Sqn was to become the first Allied unit to operate jet aircraft was very welcome. We were extremely pleased and excited, and felt very privileged to be chosen to operate this unique type of aircraft. After an introduction to the Meteor, we were briefed for our first flights. We clustered around the cockpit as Wg Cdr Wilson went through the drills, explaining the instruments and the aircraft's flying characteristics. This conversion briefing seemed rather sparse, especially as there were very few Meteor Is available. However, we felt confident, if a little overawed, at the prospect of being chosen to fly such a novel aircraft and the honour accorded to No. 616 Sqn.

Twenty-four pilots successfully converted to the aircraft, and 'they never scratched an aircraft'. It was a remarkable achievement, and testament to the training, leadership and professionalism of those involved. The unit then moved from Culmhead to its new base at Manston. On 21 July the first two Meteor Is (the non-operational EE213 and EE214) arrived at the Kent base. Finally, on 27 July, one flight was declared operational on the Meteor I.

LEHR- UND ERPROBUNGSKOMMANDO WACHTEL

The 'Wachtel Training and Test Command' was activated in April 1943 under the command of Oberst Max Wachtel. This unit, dedicated to the training of V1 launch crews, was deployed at the Zempin test range near Peenemünde, with a second training catapult being built on the Baltic coast. This start up outfit provided a solid base for the formation of *Flak-Regiment* 155(W), the unit responsible for the launching of all V1s from France – the 'W' in its designation stood for *Werfer*, or 'launcher', and not Wachtel.

Flak-Regiment 155(W) was organised along the general lines of a normal Luftwaffe flak regiment, being sub-divided into *Abteilungen* (battalions), *Batterien* (batteries) and *Zuge* (platoons). *Abteilungen* I, II, III and IV controlled the firing units, whilst *Abteilung* V was responsible for communications. Each individual *Abteilung* comprised four firing and two supply *Batterien*. In turn each firing *Batterie* controlled three *Zuge*, which comprised two firing sites and their crews. Thus the *Zug* consisted of three launchers, the *Batterie* six, the *Abteilung* 18 and the full regiment 72 launchers. Each launch ramp was manned by around 50 personnel, with the regiment as a whole totalling 6,500 men.

At the end of July 1943 training began in earnest at Zempin. The 14th Company of the Luftwaffe Air Signals Experimental Regiment set up a series of radar sites along a 155-mile stretch of the Baltic Coast, which in turn meant that all V1 launches could be tracked and vital flight data collected. On 15 August *Lehr- und Erprobungskommando* Wachtel began its training. Not only were the flak troops being trained to fire the V1, they were also assigned to the major companies responsible for the weapon's construction. This gave them a deeper understanding of the V1's inner workings and systems.

This *Bumskopf* missile was filmed moments after launch in October 1943, the round being one of two used by *Flak-Regiment* 155(W) for training purposes. Milliseconds later it would crash into the sandy dunes around Brusterot, northwest of Königsberg. These inert rounds were ballasted to simulate a fully loaded V1. (Author's Collection)

On 1 September *Flak-Regiment* 155(W) moved to Brusterort, northwest of Königsberg. It was hoped that all V1 training would be complete by the beginning of October, but a large number of personnel had yet to report for duty. The Fi 103 was a new weapon that required high quality operators, and at this stage of the war they were in short supply, being jealously guarded by all commands. Frontline COs were loath to release their best men, and even though their orders could not be ignored, they delayed their transfer for as long as possible. As a result of this friction *Flak-Regiment* 155(W) failed to reach full strength until February 1944.

Yet despite these problems the crews in training had completed three weeks of instruction and launched two ballasted dummy missiles (nicknamed *Bumskopf* (blockhead)) into the dunes near Brusterot by the end of October. After firing the dummies, the crews returned to Zempin and launched a live Fi 103 with a ballasted warhead. They were then sent back to Brusterot to continue their training with *Bumskopf* missiles.

While the training was moving forward, its progress was greatly hampered by the top-secret priority given to the project. Visual aides and illustrations were not allowed, and crews could not take any notes. They were also restricted in their training owing to the lack of missiles. The pre-production Fi 103 V variants were nearly exhausted, and there were no new examples of the M-series (part of the second batch of pre-production models before the final mass produced combat ready G-series came off the assembly lines) available for use. In mid-September the Volkswagen factory at Fallersleben began series production of the V1, but it could only manage two missiles per day. This pathetic output could not meet the training requirements, greatly hampering the whole training process.

In just three short months of training the four combat battalions of *Flak-Regiment* 155(W) each learned how to assemble, mount and launch a V1 successfully. All weapons were delivered to their launch sites by truck in a partially dismantled state. The missile was then reassembled, with the wings being fitted, along with the warhead

Oberst Max Wachtel (the officer wearing the peaked cap looking at the camera) is present during the preparations for the launch of an Fi 103A-1 flying bomb in the field just a few miles from the French coast. As can clearly be seen, this mobile site has been well camouflaged with foliage taken from nearby trees. *Flak-Regiment* 155(W)'s tried to place launchers near tree lines or within wooded areas whenever possible, thus shielding their presence from low-flying Allied fighter-bombers. RAF and USAAF pilots, wary of deadly German flak traps in the Pas-de-Calais, found these sites hard to locate as a result, which may explain the casual nature and unconcern the crew and their commanding officer seem to be exhibiting in this photograph. (Author's Collection)

V1 ON LAUNCH RAIL

A V1 is depicted here ready for launch. The Walter WR 2.3 *Schlitzrohrschleuder* ramp was constructed in six to eight modular sections that when combined reached a length of between 36 and 49m (118–160ft). Most of the modified V1 sites were well camouflaged, which made them both hard to find and difficult for 2nd TAF units to destroy. Note the *Anlaßgerät* (launch device) mounted aside the rear starboard fuselage of the missile, which included a variety of electrical connectors, safe and arming connections and other necessary triggering devices. The *Anlaßgerät* was controlled remotely from a nearby bunker.

and fuses. Prior to fuelling, the autopilot and control servo units would be checked. The flying bomb was then fuelled and compressed air bottles filled, after which it was moved to a special non-magnetic building parallel to the firing ramp and pointed in the direction of flight.

One of the early problems with the V1 was with the compass. All ferrous-metal structures have magnetic properties. The weapon was fabricated from sheet steel, and during the manufacturing process the molecules in the steel would align themselves with the earth's magnetic field. This built-in magnetism would affect any compass and cause the aircraft to fly off-course. There was, however, a very primitive solution to this problem. After the missile was finally assembled at the launching point, it was then taken into a specially built non-magnetic building. Inside the hanger crews carefully aligned the airframe onto the magnetic heading it was meant to fly. Then, using wooden mallets, personnel would beat those parts around the fuselage near the compass. This caused the molecules in the sheet-steel structure to realign themselves with the Earth's magnetic field, and in the direction of the line of flight. The compass would then be adjusted to compensate for wind drift and the ground speed calculated to enable the flight log to be set to the correct range.

With missile preparations in hand, other crewmembers would ready the launching ramp. Some 45m (156ft) long, the ramp rose to an elevated height of 4.9m (16ft) at the end. Resting on a concrete base, it was constructed from eight pre-fabricated sections, each supported at the higher end by a metal A-frame. The heart of the launching ramp was the firing tube. This ran up the entire length of the ramp. Inside the tube a cast iron firing piston was placed. Shaped like a dumb-bell, it carried a lug, which projected out of the tube. When the V1 was lowered onto the ramp the lug engaged the U-shaped launching shoe attached to the underside of the flying bomb.

With the V1 ready for launch, it was then loaded onto a *Dampferzeuger* catapult trolley and moved to the base of the ramp. There, it was lifted and lowered onto the launching cradle, which was positioned over the lug projecting from the firing piston.

While all this was going on other crewmembers would be preparing the launching ramp for firing. A great deal of force was required in order to power the cast iron firing piston forward. German scientists had decided that the best way to generate that kind of explosive energy was by mixing the reactive chemicals *Z-Stoff* (calcium permanganate) and *T-Stoff* (80 per cent hydrogen peroxide) together. The high-pressure steam that resulted would in turn drive the piston.

A GI examines a pile of cast iron firing pistons. The lug on top of the piston can be clearly seen. This was designed to engage a U-shaped shoe located on the underside of the V1, and it would power the missile to the end of the ramp during the launch sequence. (NARA)

With all the pre-launching checks made and complete, non-essential personnel would be withdrawn to positions well clear of the ramp. Early trainees soon discovered how unreliable the V1 really was, with many crashing shortly after takeoff. The firing crew, along with the site commander, would then man the concrete firing bunker located alongside the ramp. Here, the launching sequence would be initiated.

First, compressed air would push petrol from the missile's fuel tank into the pulse-jet burners. There, it was mixed with air and ignited with the spark from a conventional spark plug. Exploding into the life, the pulse-jet would vibrate and howl. As the power surged, compressed air would simultaneously force the *T-Stoff* and *Z-Stoff* rocket fuels into the combustion chamber mounted at the base of the launch ramp. Once in the chamber these two highly incompatible agents decomposed almost instantly, producing super heated steam and oxygen at high pressure.

In order to get the V1 airborne, the weapon needed to have attained a speed of 250mph by the time it reached the end of the ramp. To achieve that speed both the pulse-jet and firing piston had to provide the required energy in concert. As the pressure grew from both the thrust of the pulse-jet and firing piston, the V1 would be pushed hard against the steel bolt holding both it and the launching cradle in place. Unable to hold back the two violent forces, the steel bolt would finally shear, sending the firing piston and V1 racing down the ramp. According to German figures, the launch velocity of an operational V1 was 105 metres (340ft) per second. Thus the missile was launched in just under one second. As it left the ramp the firing piston would release from the V1 and slam into the ground some distance away.

By late October 1943 most of the training was complete. The new *Flak-Regiment* 155(W) battalions were then transferred to France. There, they would assist in the preparation of the missile bases and await the arrival of their new weapons. Their appearance in France almost coincided with the first Allied air attacks on three of the permanent ski launch sites near Ligescourt, which took place on 5 December 1943.

These attacks would continue well into May 1944. The Luftwaffe's original plan to build a series of hardened V1 launch sites proved untenable, as most, if not all, were identified and bombed. By D-Day, of the 96 launch sites completed, 83 had been damaged beyond use – only two would ever see combat. In many ways the Allied bombing campaign helped the Germans, as with their first plan of attack now turned to rubble, they were forced to design a launch site that was more survivable. For the newly minted missile men of *Flak-Regiment* 155(W), history was about to be made.

An Fi 103A-1 is loaded onto a Walter WR 2.3 launch ramp. Mounted on a *Zubringerwagon* loading trolley, the fully armed missile would be pushed to the end of the ramp and then carefully slid into place. (National Museum of the United States Air Force)

ANDREW McDOWALL

Andrew McDowall began his RAF career as a sergeant pilot with No. 602 Sqn, Royal Auxiliary Air Force. Born in 1913 in Kirkinner, Wigtownshire, in Scotland, he was working as a Clydeside engineer when he was called up at the outbreak of war. McDowall duly became one of the most successful pilots flying the Spitfire I during the air fighting of 1940. Indeed, he claimed 11 aircraft destroyed, two shared destroyed and two probables between 23 July and 6 November that year. Awarded the Distinguished Flying Medal on 8 October 1940, followed by a Bar to this award two months later, McDowall was commissioned in November of that year and posted to Hurricane I-equipped No. 245 Sqn in Northern Ireland as a flight commander in April 1941.

Andrew Mc Dowall (Author's collection)

Rested in July 1941, he was then sent to No. 52 OTU as Officer Commanding 'B' Squadron. Remaining in this position until April 1942, McDowell was posted to command Spitfire VB-equipped No. 232 Sqn upon its reformation. Five months later he was transferred to the staff of No. 13 Group. McDowall subsequently became a service test pilot with Gloster Aircraft, flying the new Meteor from late 1943.

In June 1944 No. 616 Sqn became the first unit in Fighter Command to implement the upgrading of the commanding officer's rank from squadron leader to wing commander. As a seasoned Meteor pilot, recently promoted Wg Cdr McDowall was the obvious choice for the post of squadron commander, replacing then CO Sqn Ldr Leslie Watts (who reverted to being a flight commander). He would lead the squadron through the entire V1 campaign, and be the first commander to bring Allied jet fighters to the continent while flying with the 2nd TAF. McDowall's solitary victory claim with the Meteor came on 24 April 1945 when he destroyed a Ju 88 on the ground at an airfield in Germany.

He returned to the UK just before war's end, whereupon he joined Rolls-Royce as a test pilot. McDowell conducted numerous flight trials with the company's jet engines, and in November 1945 he wrote off one of two Lockheed YP-80 jets that had been sent to the UK for testing after it suffered a fractured engine fuel pipe. Later transferring to Gloster as a staff test pilot, McDowall would receive an Air Force Cross for his work with the company. Eventually retiring in Derby, Wg Cdr Andrew McDowall passed away on 26 November 1981.

MAX WACHTEL

Oberst Max Wachtel, holder of the *Ritterkreuz* (Knight's Cross of the Iron Cross), the German Cross in Gold and the *Kriegsverdienstkreuz* (Military/War Merit Cross) with swords, was born on 6 June 1897 in Rostock.

He began his military career as an artillery officer in World War I, and in 1936 joined the flak arm of Germany's 'new army'. In August 1939 he held the rank of Commander 1st Battery, *Flak-Regiment* 704(v) in Breslau. During the invasion of France in 1940, *Flak-Regiment* 704(v) was under the staff control of *Flak-Regiment* 103, 2nd *Flak Korps*, and was deployed alongside the 'General Göring' Regiment in the 9th and 17th Flak Divisions. After the campaign Wachtel commanded a reserve detachment of the 224th *Eisenbahn* (Railway mounted) Flak Unit. In April 1941 he took command of the No. 1 Flak Training and Research and Testing Detachment at Rerik, on the Baltic. By June 1942 Wachtel was commander of the Trials Regiment/FAS 1, and at the same time leader of Training Group Luftgau FAS 1.

Two months later he was involved in Operation *Klabautermann* in the Lake Ladoga/Leningrad area of the eastern front. There, he commanded a regiment that comprised two flotillas of flak ships. Wachtel was subsequently transferred to Cherbourg, in France, and spent the winter of 1942–43 guarding U-boats as they transited to and from the harbour. From March 1943 he became leader of the Instructional Group for the Course Commander/FAS 1. This was followed on 12 May with a posting to the Luftwaffe Trials Team at Peenemünde. On 15 August Wachtel would receive his most significant and historical command when he was put in charge of *Flak-Regiment* 155(W), the cover name given to the world's first cruise missile-equipped unit. By now an Oberst, Wachtel would remain in this post until May 1945.

Post-war, he would become the director of Frankfurt airport in 1960. Wachtel passed away on 18 June 1982.

Max Wachtel (Eddie Creek)

COMBAT

On 12 June 1944 Oberst Wachtel, head of *Flak-Regiment* 155(W), addressed his commanders:

> After months of waiting, the hour has come for us to open fire! Today, your wait and your work will have their reward. The order to open fire has been issued. Now that our enemy is trying to secure at all costs his foothold on the Continent, we approach our task supremely confident in our weapons. As we launch them today, and in the future, let us always bear in mind the destruction and the suffering wrought by the enemy's terror bombing. Soldiers! *Führer* and Fatherland look to us, they expect our crusade to be an overwhelming success. As our attack begins, our thoughts linger fondly and faithfully upon our native German soil. Long live our Germany! Long live our Fatherland! Long live our *Führer*!

Much was expected of Wachtel's men and the new V1. Hitler was confident the death, destruction and humiliation to follow would demoralise the Allies to such a degree that the British government would topple and a call for negotiations to the end the war would follow. Fortunately for the Allies, Hitler's strategic military thinking was flawed and, in this case, blinded by vengeance.

The battle against the V1 had begun long before the first missile was launched. As previously noted, Operation *Crossbow*, which commenced on 5 December 1943, was the opening salvo in a long and protracted campaign. For the pilots of No. 616 Sqn, their battle against the V1 began on 22 June 1944 when 20 Spitfire VIIs provided fighter escort for an identical number of Lancasters sent to bomb the V1 storage site at Wizernes. This was followed two days later by another escort mission for Lancasters and Halifaxes bombing launch sites in the Pas-de-Calais. In addition to the these

operations, No. 616 Sqn was also fully involved supporting the Normandy landings, and all the while it was sending a steady stream of pilots to Farnborough for training on the new Meteor I.

The first V1 to be shot down by a British fighter fell on the night of 8/9 May. While flying a night intruder sortie (2305 hrs to 0100 hrs), Flg Off Bob Barckley of No 3 Sqn spotted a 'bright light' in the Le Havre area. He quickly set off in pursuit in his Tempest V:

> I thought some idiot had left his navigation lights on, so I positioned myself behind it and eventually attacked it west of Le Havre. At the time I was not aware that it was a V1, and my logbook refers to it as a 'jet-ship', which showed a degree of prescience on my part.

Of course Barckley's V1 was not part of any attack, as the opening night of the assault on London was still more than a month away. What he had intercepted was obviously a missile that had been test-fired by *Flak-Regiment* 155(W). Barckley would ultimately down 12 V1s, and share in the destruction of a 13th, between 18 June and 29 August. A second 'Diver' followed when a Beaufighter crew from No 68 Sqn claimed a 'jet-ship' on the night of 9/10 May. The next phase in the battle against the V1 was about to begin.

A V1 plunges earthward towards Piccadilly, in the London borough of Westminster, on 22 June 1944. Piccadilly suffered 29 V1 missile hits during the vengeance weapon campaign. (NARA)

Streaking over the English Channel, a London-bound Fi 103A-1 heads towards the waiting guns and fighters of the anti-Diver defence system during the summer of 1944. With a speed of close to 400mph, the unpredictability of English weather and the missile's small size (which is emphasised in this amazing aerial photograph), the V1 was difficult to both acquire and track. (NARA)

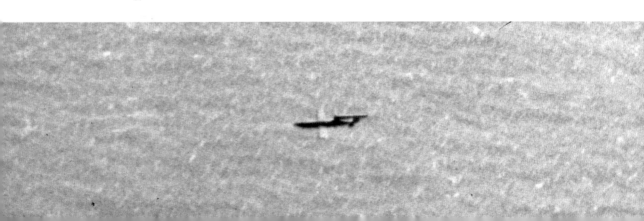

As previously described, the initial salvo on 12 June was a failure, prompting Lord Cherwell (Chief Scientific Advisor to the Prime Minister) to announce 'the mountain hath groaned and brought forth a mouse'. On the night of 12/13 June *Flak-Regiment* 155(W) had just ten ramps operational, including the one operated by V1 crewmember Unteroffizier Otto Neuchel. Much to his frustration, Neuchel's ramp suffered a piston release failure, leaving him and his crew with little option but to stand idly by and watch as adjacent sites opened the attack. Between 0330 hrs and 0400 hrs ten V1s were fired, Neuchel recalling that 'six of the ten shots went as planned, but four failed. The flying bombs fell to earth just after firing, sending us diving for cover.'

Six bombs were on their way to London. Two would plunge into the English Channel, leaving four to cross the coast. Of those, three would crash into the countryside and only one would make it to London. There, it hit the railway bridge in Grove Road, Bethnal Green, at 0425 hrs. Six people were killed and a further 30 injured, nine seriously.

The sight and sound of a V1 was unforgettable. Flying at low level and high-speed, its small size created the illusion of great speed. What many people remember was the eerie way in which the flying bomb just kept going. Indifferent to anti-aircraft guns, fighters and balloons, the missile held true to its purpose, creating a new and chilling reality. Author Evelyn Waugh summed it up well in his novel *Unconditional Surrender*, describing the V1 as being 'as impersonal as a plague, as though the city were infested with enormous venomous insects'.

What began as a whimper would soon turn into a deafening roar. To battle these lifeless harbingers the British armed forces established three lines of defence. In the frontline were the 11 squadrons of the ADGB, two of which were equipped with Mosquito nightfighters – this force was later increased to 15 single-seat and eight nightfighter squadrons. The single-seat units were equipped with Tempest Vs, Typhoon IBs, Spitfire IXs, XIIs and XIVs and Mustang IIIs. The RAF also had great expectations for its newest secret weapon, the twin-jet Meteor I. Next in line were almost 200 heavy and light AAA guns in a belt across central Kent, running from the north bank of the estuary, through Tunbridge Wells to Leatherhead in the west. Finally, on the eastern outskirts of London, 480 barrage balloons stood guard.

On the night of 16/17 June the battle was joined in earnest as 55 launchers fired 244 missiles (including 50 launched at the port cities of Portsmouth and Southampton), of which 45 crashed after takeoff. Some 155 were sighted by personnel manning the defences, with 144 crossing the coast and 73 penetrating to Greater London. A total of 33 V1s were shot down, 12 by fighters and 21 by AAA.

For the pilots of No. 616 Sqn it would be another month-and-half before they would be able to join the fight proper. By 27 July the squadron had six Meteor Is on strength at its new Manston home in east Kent. One flight was declared operational with four aircraft (the other two jets were training machines EE213/YQ-A and EE214/YQ-B, which were easily recognised

After a successful launch, another V1 streaks towards London. Only about a quarter of the total number of Fi 103s expended during the summer of 1944 impacted in the target area. Of the 8,617 V1s launched, 1,052 crashed immediately after takeoff. If this had been an Allied weapon system such a high failure rate would have rendered the V1 unacceptable for frontline use. (Author's Collection)

by their yellow undersides that earned the nickname 'Yellow Bellies'). Taking command of the flight was Wg Cdr Andrew McDowall (it was customary for RAF squadrons equipped with multi-engined aircraft to be led by a wing commander). Sqn Ldr Les Watts remained with the unit to command the Spitfire flight. Also joining No. 616 Sqn at this time was Wg Cdr Hugh 'Willie' Wilson, who had been one of the pioneering Meteor I pilots at the RAE. He arrived with his own personalised aircraft, EE224/HJW.

The task of flying the RAF's first operational sortie in a jet aircraft fell to Canadian Flg Off W. H. 'Mac' McKenzie, who took off at 1430 hrs on 27 July for an uneventful patrol near Ashford. More flights were made later that afternoon (by Wg Cdr McDowall in EE215/YQ-C, Wg Cdr Wilson in HJW, Flg Off Rodger in EE219/YQ-D and WO Wilkes in EE213/YQ-A) and again no V1s were spotted. However, two pilots did come close to claiming No. 616 Sqn's first victories with the Meteor I, as detailed in the following entry from the unit diary:

> Sqn Ldr Watts (EE213/YQ-A) was unfortunate in having trouble with his guns as he was about to open the squadron's Diver score near Ashford. Flg Off Dean (EE215/YQ-C) sighted one Diver and followed in line astern at 405mph. He had closed to within 1,000 yards of the bomb, estimated to be flying at 390mph, when he was turned back by control owing to the proximity of balloons. Pilots are convinced that given favourable weather and good plots nothing can prevent the Meteor knocking down the latest Axis weapon.

A V1 heads northeast over Kentish countryside, London-bound. Of the missiles shot down by ADGB fighters, about 90 per cent went down out of control and exploded when they hit the ground. Roughly ten per cent detonated in mid-air, and if the attacking pilot was closer than 150 yards when the V1 exploded, the conflagration could damage or, in some cases, destroy his aircraft. (NARA)

The battle was joined. Air Marshal Sir Roderic Hill, the man responsible for rushing the Meteor I into service, later wrote:

> I decided to match jet against jet by trying it out against the flying bomb. At first only a few of these aircraft were available, and various problems, including that of limited endurance, had to be overcome before we could get the full benefit out of the Meteor's great speed.

Meteor YQ-K (serial unknown) is seen at Manston hooked up to its accumulator trolley and ready for flight in August 1945. (Author's Collection)

By mid-July *Flak-Regiment* 155(W) had fired 4,361 missiles, including 90 air-launched weapons. Of those 2,934 were logged by the defences, 1,693 escaped destruction and 1,270 got through to the capital, with the balance of the survivors falling elsewhere. ADGB and AA Command shot down 1,241, with 924 credited to the fighters, 261 to the guns and 55 to barrage balloons.

As successful as the defences were, the V1 attacks were beginning to have an effect. Panic gripped the residents of London, and under a government plan more than 360,000 women, children and the infirm were evacuated. Hitler was thrilled by the press accounts, and he ordered the Luftwaffe to expand its efforts. Churchill was not impressed, and demanded more action be taken to silence the missile batteries. Air attacks against the modified sites (codenamed *Noball*) were stepped up, but because these sites were easily camouflaged and quick to move, the results were disappointing. It even reached the point where the Allies considered using US Marine Corps squadrons flying F4U Corsairs that were armed with unguided, and as yet untried, 'Tiny Tim' rocket projectiles to attack the modified sites.

Poor weather curtailed Meteor operations following No. 616 Sqn's rather muted combat debut on 27 July, flying finally resuming on 2 August when four anti-Diver patrols were carried out between Ashford and Robertsbridge. The new aircraft attracted a great deal of attention, and the squadron continued to receive visitors each day. One of those was veteran fighter ace Wg Cdr Roly Beaumont, Officer Commanding No. 150 Tempest Wing (credited with 32 V1s shot down). He was rather underwhelmed by the Meteor I:

> It ought to have been an impressive experience but somehow it was not. The low, thin fuselage and blunt nose profile was not enhanced by an awkward looking high tail, with two bulges at mid-wing on either side which were distinctly more reminiscent of beer barrels that of aerodynamically refined engine nacelles.

For the pilots of No. 616 Sqn the frustration of having not yet claimed a V1 victory when the other units in ADGB seemed to be knocking them down by the dozen was beginning to show. They had come close, and the events of 3 August would be no different, but at least this time the first shots had finally been fired in anger. While on patrol Flt Lt Mike Graves sighted a Diver and had no difficulty in overtaking it. At a range of 400–500 yards he squeezed the trigger and fired a two-second burst from his four Hispano Mk III 20mm cannons. No strikes were seen, and just as Graves manoeuvred in for a second attack a Mustang 'crashed the party' and dispatched the V1.

3 August would also prove to be the busiest day for the defenders, as *Flak-Regiment* 155(W) succeeded in launching the highest number of V1s fired in a single day. No fewer than 316 left their ramps, with 220 reaching London. Day fighters accounted for 40 V1s.

4 August would be the day that No. 616 Sqn finally opened its score. At 1545 hrs Flg Off 'Dixie' Dean was scrambled in EE216/YQ-E for an anti-Diver patrol between Ashford and Robertsbridge. Flying at 4,500ft under the guidance of Biggin Hill Control ('Kingsley 11'), Dean spotted a Diver 4–5 miles southeast of Tenterden, in Kent. From 2½ miles behind the Diver, Dean pushed the control column of his jet

forward, increasing his speed to 470mph and rapidly closed the gap. With the V1 squarely in his sights, Dean pushed the firing button but nothing happened – his 20mm cannons had jammed:

> I half expected the guns to jam because several other pilots had experienced that problem before me. I also knew that any sudden movement would upset the V1, and so when my guns failed I already had a good idea of what I should do. I just followed on in and tipped it up. When I got back to base I found that there was a small dent in my wingtip where I had hit the flying bomb. This was the only damage to the aircraft, which was serviceable again after a few hours.

Dean had sent the Diver down on its back into the ground near Tonbridge, in west Kent. The squadron diarist noted that 'This is the first pilotless aircraft to be destroyed by a jet-propelled aircraft.' But there was more to come. Shortly afterwards, at 1640 hrs, Flg Off Jock Rodger actually shot down the first V1 using his 20mm cannons:

> I sighted a Diver over Tenterden flying at 3,000ft at 340mph. I immediately attacked from dead astern and fired a two-second burst at a range of 350 yards. I saw several hits and saw petrol or oil streaming out of the Diver, which continued to fly straight and level. I fired another two-second burst from my four cannons, still from 300 yards. Both Meteor and Diver were flying at 340mph. The Diver then went down and exploded on the ground about five miles northwest of Tenterden.

Unfortunately, things did not go all No. 616 Sqn's way in the summer of 1944. The sight of the Meteor I in the skies of southern England was a surprise to many AAA gunners and fighter pilots alike. Flg Off Ian Wilson, while returning from a patrol, found himself being bounced by two Spitfires. Cannon shells ripped through his elevators, forcing him to make an emergency landing. Without elevator control, Wilson managed to nurse his fighter down by using the tailplane trim control only. It was a remarkable piece of flying considering he had had just a few hours flying time on the new jet.

AAA gun crews also had trouble identifying the Meteors, as former Gunner Ron Ford recalled:

> Control told us that there was a fast target approaching at 3,000ft. I had seen a Meteor a few days earlier, but before I could shout a warning the guns started to fire. No one noticed that it had two engines and was much bigger than a V1 – they thought it was a German aircraft. The pilot gave a remarkable display of the aircraft's manoeuvrability, and every other gun opened up on it as it took evasive action and escaped. The next day we received a message from AA Command that said 'A Meteor aircraft

A V1 impacts short of London. The Fi 103 carried two separate impact-fusing systems to detonate the warhead, as well as a backup clockwork time fuse. These proved to be highly effective, for of the first 2,700 V1s to land on British soil, only four failed to explode. Because the weapon did not bury itself deep in the ground prior to exploding, the resulting blast wave was extremely destructive, causing far more damage than the larger and more sophisticated V2 rocket. (Author's Collection)

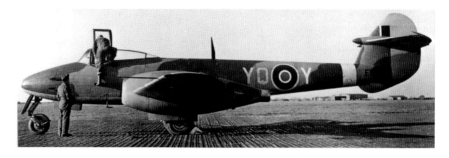

will be patrolling the Thames Estuary at noon for identification purposes only – repeat, identification purposes only.'

By 7 August No. 616 Sqn was equipped with 12 Meteor Is, which was enough to allow two flights to be declared operational with 33 pilots fully converted onto the type. The 7th would again prove to be a busy day for ADGB's fighter units, which claimed 34 V1s shot down – the majority were brought down by Tempest Vs and Mustang IIIs. No. 616 Sqn would contribute just one success to this tally when Flg Off T. D. Dean took credit for his second V1:

At approximately 0620 hrs I intercepted a Diver four miles east of Robertsbridge. The Diver was flying at 1,000ft at an estimated speed of 390mph. I came into attack line astern at 400mph and opened fire with all four cannons at 700 yards. I continued firing in short bursts, closing in to 500 yards. Strikes were seen and pieces fell away from the Diver's starboard wing. Finally, I broke away, having expended my ammunition, and I saw the Diver go down in a shallow dive. It was not possible to see if the Diver crashed owing to prevailing ground mist. It was later confirmed by the ROC [Royal Observer Corps] that the Diver had crashed at 0625 hrs.

As this success graphically proves, by 7 August the difficulties initially experienced with the Meteor I's Hispano cannons had finally been overcome. In the rush to get the aircraft into operational service, there had been little time to complete the jet's weapon firing trials. This in turn resulted in frequent gun jamming, which was caused by up-draughts within the under-fuselage ejector slots that prevented the empty shell cases from being discarded.

During No. 616 Sqn's investigation into the cannon jamming problems, pilots were required to carry out numerous gunnery tests, and a favourite area for strafing runs was the mud flats of the Thames Estuary. Pilots quickly found the Meteor's diving speed built up rapidly, and it proved to be too fast for comfort. The Mk I was not fitted with speed brakes, so pilots were forced to come in at a much shallower angle of attack that was in fact almost parallel with the ground. This resulted in the projectiles churning up a shower of mud that several Meteors actually flew through. The jets subsequently returned to Manston with dented and torn engine nacelles, wing leading edges and fuselage undersides.

On 10 August six patrols were made, with 12 pilots scrambling under 'Kingsley 11' Control. During an afternoon patrol Flg Off T. D. Dean completed his hat-trick of V1 successes when he shot down a Diver near Ashford:

ENGAGING THE ENEMY

Downing a V1 proved to be a hazardous task. Pilots quickly learned that they were in fact engaging a live bomb, and not just another enemy aircraft. When attacking from astern and at close range the results were wildly unpredictable. A single 20mm cannon shell could easily penetrate the V1's outer shell, and when it struck the weapon's warhead the resulting explosion was often catastrophic for both aircraft. The end result of 1,870lb of high explosives erupting in mid-air was an immense fireball and a cloud of debris, into which the pursuer was forced to fly.

While the first V1 to be brought down by a Meteor was not shot down by cannon fire, the remaining 11 credited to No. 616 Sqn were, using the Meteor I's quartet of nose-mounted 20mm cannons. In order to negate the missile's high speed, a pair of jets would climb to an altitude well

above the V1's average height of 1,000–3,000ft. Once the incoming weapon had survived the hail of flak from the guns located on the coast it was the Meteor's turn. Vectored by radar, the pilot would then get into the right position and altitude, open the throttles and begin scanning the terrain below. Once the V1 was spotted, he would trade height for speed. Diving at speeds in excess of 400mph, the pilot would position his Meteor above and astern of the V1.

Because the Meteor's guns were mounted in the nose and not the wings, the pilot did not have to worry about converging fire. Engaging the missile at long-range once he had the V1 in his state-of-the-art Ferranti Mk II gyroscopic gunsight, pilots routinely registered hits from 700 yards astern, but in most cases the damage was done at the more lethal range of 300–100 yards.

While under 'Kingsley 11' Control I saw a Diver coming west from Folkestone. The Diver was flying at 5,000ft at an estimated speed of 200mph. Diving down from 6,000ft, I intercepted the Diver as it came out of the gun belt northwest of Folkestone at 2105 hrs. I made two orbits of the Diver and then came in to attack. No other aircraft were seen in the vicinity at the time. Two bursts of cannon were fired, one one-second burst at ten degrees deflection, range 200 yards, and one two-second burst from line astern at 100 yards. Pieces were seen to fall off the wings and the Diver rolled onto its back and commenced a spin to the ground. While the Diver was spinning down, two other aircraft, believed to be Tempests, were seen to cannon the Diver, which crashed and exploded five miles northwest of Ashford.

Just as No. 616 Sqn was getting into its operational stride the number of V1 launches began to decrease owing to problems with the re-supplying of weapons and a gradual reduction in the number of launch areas in the Pas-de-Calais. As previously noted, *Flak-Regiment* 155(W) succeeded in launching 316 V1s on 3 August, but it then suffered a gradual attrition owing to direct air attacks. Ultimately, the unit averaged just 34 launches per day during the course of the summer campaign. By mid-August Allied troops had crossed the River Seine and were making rapid progress towards the V1 launch sites. The order soon went out to *Flak-Regiment* 155(W) to move all surplus equipment towards Antwerp and bases in the Netherlands. On 9 August *Abteilung* IV was ordered to pull back, followed by *Abteilung* III the following day. Finally, the *Korps* headquarters was forced to move on 18–19 August, leaving just *Abteilung* I to continue launching V1s from northern France.

This was the official report created by No. 616 Sqn's Intelligence Officer following WO Sid Woodacre's V1 victory on 17 August 1944 near Faversham. (Graham Pitchfork)

During No. 616 Sqn's period of increased operational activity on anti-Diver patrols, the unit's remaining Spitfire VIIs continued flying shipping sweeps and weather reconnaissance missions. The latter usually took place over Belgium and extended along the French coast from Cherbourg to Ostend. By 14 August, however, the last of the piston-engined fighters had been retired, leaving No. 616 Sqn as the Allies' first all-jet fighter unit (it was equipped with 14 of the original 20 Meteor Is).

In mid-August the squadron started to use High Halden Advanced Landing Ground (ALG), seven miles southwest of Ashford, as a temporary airfield. Two aircraft and a small servicing party were positioned there each day. Sadly, on 15 August, the RAF and No. 616 Sqn suffered its first jet loss and pilot casualty. Taking off from Manston in the late afternoon, Flt Sgt D. A. Gregg was to fly EE226 (which had been with the unit for only

CONSOLIDATED DIVER REPORT.

No. 616 SQUADRON   SECRET

W/O Woodacre T.S.   Date:- 17.8.44.

        While on 'Anti Diver' Patrol under Biggin Control W/O Woodacre saw a 'DIVER' coming in from direction of north of Dover.

2.   'DIVER' was intercepted by 'Meteor' 3 miles south of Canterbury and estimated flying at 400 m.p.h. at height of 1500 feet.

3.   One 'Mustang' aircraft was seen 700/1000 yards astern of the 'DIVER' but did not fire.

4.   W/O Woodacre had no difficulty in overtaking both Mustang and Diver then attacked and fired three short bursts at range of 200 yards. Strikes were seen on the root of starboard wing of 'DIVER' which rolled over and went down and was seen to explode on ground 4 miles south of Faversham at 07.08 hours.

CLAIM: 1 'Diver destroyed by W/O Woodacre T.S.
SQUADRON - 616 Squadron   AIRCRAFT   Meteor Mk. 1
CALL SIGN   HUGO   33   WEATHER 10/10ths cloud
TIME UP: 06.45. DOWN: 07.30.   3000ft. visibility good.
NO. OF ROUNDS FIRED 50 RDS.PER GUN.

....
T.S. Woodacre w/o
Intelligence Officer   T.S. Woodacre   W/O
616 Squadron   616 Squadron

                    Confirmed!

48 hours) directly to High Halden and join the readiness section there, but he never made it. Unable to locate the small airstrip, he diverted to the ALG at nearby Great Chart, near Ashford. Unfortunately, his attempt to land ended in tragedy. The 21-year-old pilot was buried in Nottingham.

Putting this tragedy behind it, No. 616 Sqn would experience one of its busiest days on the 16th. After an uneventful scramble and patrol, Flg Off Bill McKenzie had his gear down, ready for landing, when control reported Divers coming in. Pushing the throttles forward, McKenzie (EE225) flew five miles southwest of Ashford and began orbiting at 3,000ft. Shortly after he spotted a Diver, but he was not alone:

I positioned to 700 yards behind and 500ft below the Diver. A Mustang [flown by Polish Diver ace Flt Sgt Stanislaw Rudowski of No. 306 Sqn] attacked from line astern and fired from 250 yards. No strikes were observed and the Diver continued on a straight and level course. The Mustang then pulled upwards and broke away. I immediately attacked from astern from 400 yards and fired a four-second burst. Strikes were seen all over the Diver and the starboard wing fell off. The Diver then rolled over onto its back and exploded when it hit the ground approximately eight miles east of Maidstone at 0940 hrs.

This was a shared victory, and Rudowski complained that the Meteor pilot had actually attacked him, damaging his aircraft! At 1833 hrs Belgian Flg Off Prule Mullenders added to the score with a V1 shot down in the vicinity of Ashford. The day ended with Wg Cdr Andy McDowall damaging two V1s in the Tenterden area. Strikes were seen on the Divers, but McDowall had to break away both times owing the proximity of the balloon barrage.

17 August would see the squadron's second loss of life as an all-jet unit. After completing a late-afternoon patrol Meteor I EE225 was standing at dispersal when, at 1750 hrs, Flg Off Bill McKenzie inadvertently fired its cannons, damaging Wg Cdr Wilson's EE224/HJW. Four groundcrew were injured, including a Rolls-Royce representative. Unfortunately, Cpl W. M. Harding was mortally wounded, succumbing to his injuries eight days later. McKenzie was found negligent, but Wg Cdr McDowall insisted that the incident was an accident owing to aircraft malfunction, and not pilot error.

On a more positive note, the 17th would also prove to be No. 616 Sqn's most productive day in combat against the V1 menace. The action started with Flg Off J. R. Ritch RCAF flying EE217/YQ-J:

A Diver was seen flying at 2,000ft from the direction of Hastings towards Maidstone. I intercepted in the vicinity of Tenterden at 0657 hrs. Two Tempests were seen flying behind the Diver. One Tempest was seen to fire but no strikes were observed. I went in to attack and fired one long burst from line astern from 150 to 100 yards. Strikes were seen and the Diver rolled over and fell away to explode on the ground four miles south of Maidstone.

Seconds later Ritch's wingman, WO Sid Woodacre (EE218/YQ-F), used the Meteor's superior speed to overtake a Mustang and blast a V1 out of the sky:

OVERLEAF
17 August 1944 would prove to be No. 616 Sqn's big day with three Divers shot down. The first was claimed by Canadian Flg Off Jack Ritch, flying Meteor I EE217/YQ-J. The weather was 10/10ths cloud at 3,000ft and the visibility was good. 'At 0615 hrs Flg Off Ritch was on patrol (inland area) from Manston (under Biggin Control). Two Tempests were seen flying behind the Diver and one Tempest was seen to fire, with no results. I intercepted in the vicinity of Tenterden at 0654 hrs. I went into the attack and fired one long burst from line astern at 150 to 100 yards. Strikes were seen and the Diver rolled over and fell away to explode on the ground four miles south of Maidstone.' No. 616 Sqn's other V1 victories on this date were credited to WO T. S. Woodacre and Flt Sgt R. Easy at 0700 hrs and 1355 hrs respectively.

Control warned me that there was a fast contact south of Canterbury at 1,500ft, and I soon spotted it because there was a Mustang about 1,000 yards behind it, but not getting any closer. I passed the P-51 doing over 400mph and caught up with the flying bomb. We had been warned not to fly directly behind the bomb because the slipstream would slow us down a bit. Instead, we had to approach to one side and close behind to 200 yards before opening fire. I fired three short bursts at the starboard wing root and the Diver rolled over and blew up when it hit the ground south of Faversham. I could feel the blast rock my aircraft. It was very straightforward and easy. The target was flying straight and level and didn't shoot back – what more could a fighter pilot want?

This wrecked railway car full of V1s was found by British troops in Holland in the autumn of 1944. Supplying the launch sites proved problematic for the Luftwaffe in both France and the Netherlands. Allied fighter-bomber attacks were constant, and this greatly restricted the number of V1s that could be launched on any given day. (NARA)

The third V1 fell to the guns of Flt Sgt R. Easy. While orbiting High Halden, Biggin Hill Control reported three Divers were approaching Ashford at 1,000–3,000ft. Easy managed to intercept them northwest of the town:

I opened my attack from line astern with a one-second burst at 400 yards. Observing a few strikes on the starboard wing root, I closed in and fired from slightly below and astern at 250–200 yards. Three more two-second bursts were fired and strikes were observed all over the Diver. More strikes were seen when I fired another burst of two seconds. Diver fell away to starboard and was seen to explode in a field close to Canterbury/Maidstone railway line at 1355 hrs.

Two days later Flg Off G. N. Hobson nearly scored a double while flying EE217/YQ-J, but had to share his second V1 when a Tempest crashed the party. After claiming his first success over Ashford at 0646 hrs, he spotted a second V1 south of Tenterden. He attacked the Diver from its starboard side with a five-second burst, and moments later a Tempest finished it off with a pass from line astern. At 2050 hrs that evening Flt Sgt P. G. Watts was scrambled, and 20 minutes later he shot down a V1 in the West Malling area. 19 August ended with Flt Sgt B. Cartmel claiming a V1 damaged in the Chilham area.

A further nine days would pass before No. 616 Sqn had the chance to add to its score as the number of V1s reaching Britain at this time was beginning to drop off. Allied ground forces were rapidly overrunning the launch sites, and it would only be a matter of days before the first phase of the V1 offensive would come to an end. On 28 August Flg Off G. N. Hobson (in EE217/JQ-J) and Flt Sgt E. Epps combined to down a V1. Scrambled at 1625 hrs, both pilots were ordered to orbit Tenterden. What followed turned out to be a classic example of the Meteor I's superior low-level speed in comparison with its piston-engined counterparts, Hobson recalling:

OPPOSITE
Gun camera footage of a V1 exploding in mid-air. Pursuing fighter pilots quickly learned that engaging an Fi 103 too closely could end in disaster. Five pilots were killed outright by exploding V1s, and another 13 pilots/navigators are believed to have been killed in crashes following damage inflicted on their aircraft by detonating missiles. (NARA)

Three Tempests were seen 2,000 yards behind and on the same course as the Diver. The Tempests seemed to be losing ground and gradually fell behind. I passed over the Tempests and fired two three-second bursts at 300 yards from behind and slightly above the Diver. Continuing to close, I fired one three-second burst from 100 yards. The Diver immediately spun to earth and exploded. No other aircraft was seen at the time of the attack as I broke away. I saw another Meteor breaking away to port.

That other Meteor was flown by Flt Sgt Eddie Epps, who was also in on the attack: 'I attacked from level behind and opened fire at 300 yards with one short burst. Strikes were seen as the Diver dipped onto its starboard wing.' The V1 was listed as having crashed at 1658 hrs in the Tenterden area.

For the pilots of No. 616 Sqn, 29 August was the last time they would battle the V1. It was a day that ended with one flying bomb shot down and another Meteor written off. At 1415 hrs Flg Off H. Miller scored his first and No. 616 Sqn's last V1 victory in the Sittingbourne area. As with most intercepts, the airspace was a crowded place, as Miller recalled in his combat report:

Two Tempests were seen 600 yards behind the Diver. Both fired but no strikes were observed. Owing to the Tempests flying line astern of the Diver I was forced to make a beam attack from port, and fired three two-second bursts at 100 yards. Strikes were seen on the port wing. I again attacked, this time from above and slightly behind at 400 yards. I observed strikes from my fire and the Diver rolled over and exploded.

The Meteor I's Achilles heel was its short range and endurance. On this day Wg Cdr Andy McDowall was flying EE222/YQ-G on a anti-Diver patrol when he ran out of fuel and crash-landed south of Manston. Following the normal Spitfire forced landing procedure, he came in wheels up. It was a mistake. The smooth clean lines of the Meteor's belly caused it to careen across the field and crash through the hedges at the end of the field. Although Wg Cdr McDowall escaped this incident with only a few minor facial cuts, his jet was a write-off.

The last anti-Diver patrol of the day was flown by Flt Lt Dennis Barry in EE227/YQ-Y, with no results. Some 26 V1s had been shot down by single-seat fighters on 29 August.

At 0400 hrs on 1 September *Abteilung* I fired its final V1 from France. For the missile men of *Flak-Regiment* 155(W) the first phase of their campaign with the Fi 103 had come to an end. The combined Allied air and ground attacks had rendered them

incapable of conducting further ground-launched attacks. After a slow start, the unit had achieved impressive results in the face of mounting adversity. Between 13 June and 5 September *Flak-Regiment* 155(W) and aircraft from He 111-equipped III. *Gruppe* of *Kampfgeschwader* 3 (400 were air-launched at night, the vast majority of them aimed at London) had launched 8,617 V1s, 1,052 of which immediately after takeoff. Some 5,913 had made it to England, and of those AA Command had downed 1,459, the balloon barrage claimed 231 and fighters (both day and night) were credited with 1,771. Approximately 2,450 missiles hit London.

This He 111H-16, coded 'CK+UE', was used during flight tests involving Fi 103 V90 at Karlshagen on 7 September 1943. Specially modified Heinkel bombers were widely used during the air-launched phase of the battle in 1944, these aircraft being fitted with FuG 101 radio altimeters and 'Lichtenstein' tail-warning radar. The added weight of the V1 and its associated equipment severely affected the He 111's already limited performance. British nightfighters claimed 22 of the specially modified Heinkels destroyed. All told III./KG 3 and KG 53 recorded 77 He 111H-22s lost to all causes while on V1 operations. (Jim Laurier)

STATISTICS AND ANALYSIS

The first phase of the V1 campaign against London had come to an end, and when phases II and III began later that year No. 616 Sqn would once again be asked to join the fight against Hitler's V-weapons.

For the RAF's first frontline jet pilots, their participation in anti-Diver operations had been a success, but only a modest one. Late to the battle, and with few aircraft available, they had managed to shoot down 12.5 V1s during the course of 260 sorties.

While their opponent could not shoot back, the V1 nevertheless proved to be a deadly adversary. Difficult to shoot down, the weapon's small size and high speed also made it hard to pick up visually. For a fighter pilot attempting to shoot down a V1, the presentation area from dead astern was just 16 sq. ft, compared with 45 sq. ft for the Fw 190. A pilot had to get in close to shoot it down, and that could prove dangerous because the V1 was, after all, a bomb waiting to explode. A single cannon shell was often enough to cause a massive explosion and possible destruction of the pursuing fighter. Fortunately for the pilots of No. 616 Sqn this never happened, but there were plenty of losses in other units. In all, 72 RAF pilots and navigators were lost to all causes during the campaign – a high number considering the V1 could not shoot back.

How did the Meteor I's anti-V1 efforts compare to the results achieved by its contemporaries? The best single-seat fighter was the Tempest V, followed by the Spitfire F XIV, in terms of the number of missiles shot down. The figures overleaf provide a snapshot in time of the effectiveness of each fighter. It must be remembered that the Meteor I did not achieve its first kill until 4 August, and the figures overleaf

OPPOSITE TOP
This illustration shows an He 111H-22 from III./KG 53 nearing the Dutch coast as it heads outbound at the start of another nocturnal V1 air-launching mission in the autumn of 1944. The newly modified Heinkels carried special equipment to carry and launch the V1, and they were also fitted with a FuG 101 radio altimeter and Lichtenstein tail warning radar. The added weight and drag severely affected the bombers' performance, making them easy prey for British nightfighters. All told, 77 He 111s were lost during the V1 air-launching campaign, with RAF nightfighters claiming 22 shot down, three damaged and four probables. The rest were lost to all causes during operations.

A group shot of No. 616 Sqn pilots taken in January 1945 while based at Colerne airfield. Pilots who scored V1 victories in this photograph are Flg Off T. D. Dean (second row, second from right), WO T. S. Woodacre (second row, eighth from right), Flg Off M. M. Mullenders (second row, tenth from right), Flt Sgt E. Epps (second row, 11th from right), Flt Sgt P. G. Watts (second row, 12th from right) and Flg Off J. K. Rodger (second row, 14th from right). Sat in the centre of the front row is the squadron CO, Wg Cdr A. McDowall DFM and Bar, while V1 killer Flg Off G. N. Hobson is sitting in the first row, first on the right, and Flt Sgt R. Easy is standing at left in the back row. (Graham Pitchfork)

do not include the total number of sorties flown by both the Tempest V and Spitfire F XIV. It must also be remembered that there were far more examples of both fighters available in the summer of 1944. Nevertheless, these statistics are illuminating, and they reveal just how effective the Tempest was at killing V1s:

15 June to 18 July 1944
Tempest V
Total V1s destroyed – 498
Sorties flown – 2,375
Kills per sortie – 0.21
Sorties per kill – 4.7
Spitfire F XIV
Total V1s destroyed – 227
Sorties flown – 2,169
Kills per sortie – 0.10
Sorties per kill – 9.5
1 to 29 August 1944
Meteor
Total V1s destroyed – 12.5
Sorties flown – 260
Kills per sortie – 0.046
Sorties per kill – 21.6

In early September the anti-Diver patrols for No. 616 Sqn came to an end. The rest of the month was spent gaining more jet experience, conducting formation flying and demonstrating their new aircraft to other Allied air and ground units. Finally, at the end of the month, the press was cleared to reveal the Meteor I's existence. Between 10 and 13 October No. 616 Sqn detached four Meteors to RAF Debden, in Essex, which was home to the USAAF's 4th Fighter Group. Whilst here, the pilots helped train their USAAF counterparts flying the Mustang who had been struggling to defend B-17s and B-24s against attacks by Me 262s and Me 163s over Germany.

During their three days at Debden the Meteor pilots conducted a number of hotly contested mock dogfights in clear skies directly over the airfield, much to the delight of the assembled USAAF servicemen on the ground.

Air power alone could not defeat the V1 threat, but it did contribute greatly to the weapon's overall demise. It was only after ground troops overran the launch sites that the V1 threat subsided. Here, British soldiers inspect a Walter *Schlitzrohrschleuder* WR 2.3 launch ramp that was wrecked by aerial bombing. (NARA)

These sorties allowed the Mustang pilots to get a better understanding of what they were up against over Germany, and the Americans freely admitted that their RAF opponents were the victors in every engagement flown thanks to the Meteor's ability to easily outrun the P-51 should it become cornered.

On 18 December No. 616 Sqn received its first new Meteor III (EE231). The first 15 Mk IIIs were powered by the same Welland engines fitted to the Mk I, so there was no real improvement in terms of performance. In fact, the most significant feature of the Mk III was a new streamlined canopy.

A little over a month later, on 20 January 1945, Meteor Mk IIIs EE235/YQ-P, EE239/YQ-Q, EE240/YQ-R and EE241/YQ-S were flown to Melsbroek airfield, near Brussels, to join the 2nd TAF. By 13 February, the first Rolls-Royce Derwent-engined (2,000lb thrust) Meteor IIIs had been collected by No. 616 Sqn. In March the Meteor was once again asked to battle the V1 when German launch sites in Holland began firing the extended range Fi 103E-1 towards London. No. 616 Sqn flew a total of 15 sorties from Andrews Field, in Essex, but failed to intercept a single missile. On the 16th of that month the aircraft strength within the unit was as follows:

4 Meteor IIIs with B.23 engines at B.58 (Melsbroek) airfield, Brussels

15 Meteor IIIs with B.37 engines at Andrew's Field, Essex

3 Meteor IIIs with B.37 engines allotted but not yet received

Finally, on 3 April No. 616 Sqn was fully equipped with 17 examples of the Derwent-engined Meteor III. Frustratingly for the unit, airborne opponents proved elusive, leaving the Meteor pilots to contend themselves with strafing ground targets. From April until VE-Day, No. 616 Sqn managed to compile a healthy score of ground targets – 42 MET (mechanised enemy transport) destroyed and 144 damaged, two locomotives destroyed and one damaged and four aircraft destroyed and three damaged.

OPPOSITE
As this map clearly shows,
ADGB's anti-Diver campaign in
the summer and early autumn of
1944 was fought exclusively in
the southeastern corner of
England. This was because the
V1 launchers were based along
the Channel coast in
northwestern France and
Belgium.

Meteor I V1 killers	
Flg Off T. D. Dean	3
Flg Off G. N. Hobson	1 and 1 shared with Tempest
Flt Sgt R. Easy	1
Flg Off H. Miller	1
Flg Off M. M. Mullenders	1
Flg Off J. R. Ritch	1
Flg Off J. K. Rodger	1
WO T. S. Woodacre	1
Flt Sgt P. G. Watts	1
Flt Sgt E. Epps	1 shared
Flg Off W. H. McKenzie	1 shared with Mustang III of No. 306 Sqn
Wg Cdr A. McDowall	2 damaged
Flt Sgt B. Cartmel	1 damaged

For the missile men of *Flak-Regiment* 155(W), their time in France had been brief. As British and Canadian ground forces moved into the Pas-de-Calais area they were forced to abandon their sites and join the general retreat. Through the chaos and constant fear of air attack, the unit managed to extract about three-quarters of its troops from France. Only Abteilung III managed to extract all of its heavy launch equipment. The regiment was reorganised around two launch battalions, with the other two being converted to regular flak units. Even though the ground-launched V1s had ceased firing, London was still under attack.

On 9 July 1944 modified He 111H-22s began air-launching V1s towards London. By 5 September III./KG 3 had expended 300 missiles against London, 90 against Southampton and 20 against Gloucester. With the launch sites in France now extinct, the air campaign was stepped up. Operating from bases in Holland, III./KG 3 was reorganised to become I./KG 53 in the autumn (the exact date has never been found in surviving Luftwaffe records). By 23 November I., II. and III./KG 53 had a combined strength of 83 He 111H-22s, 55 of which were serviceable. These aircraft would be in the vanguard of the second phase in the V1 campaign against London, which was a totally nocturnal affair.

To counter this new threat Mosquito and Beaufighter nightfighters, as well as day fighter Tempests tasked with flying after dark, were employed with great effect. Aside from destroying V1s, the British fighters would account for 22 He 111s shot down. The last launch was conducted on 14 January 1945, this phase being brought to a halt through a lack of fuel for the Heinkels. All told, 1,776 V1s had been air-

NCO technicians (right) set the 'log' of a V1 before the 'black men' of the groundcrew attach the missile to the He 111H-16 of KG 53 seen in its camouflaged dispersal bay at an airfield in the Netherlands in the autumn of 1944. (John Weal)

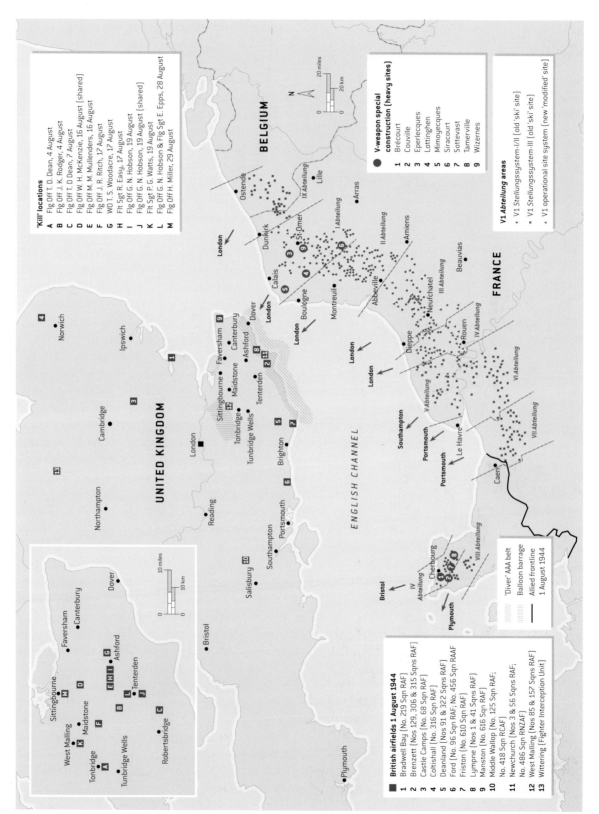

'Kill' locations

A Flg Off T. D. Dean, 4 August
B Flg Off J. K. Rodger, 4 August
C Flg Off T. D Dean, 7 August
D Flg Off W. H. McKenzie, 16 August [shared]
E Flg Off M. M. Mullenders, 16 August
F Flg Off J. R. Ritch, 17 August
G WO T. S. Woodacre, 17 August
H Flt Sgt R. Easy, 17 August
I Flg Off G. N. Hobson, 19 August
J Flg Off G. N. Hobson, 19 August [shared]
K Flt Sgt P. G. Watts, 19 August
L Flg Off G. N. Hobson & Flg Sgt E. Epps, 28 August
M Flg Off H. Miller, 29 August

V-weapon special
construction [heavy sites]

● 1 Brécourt
   2 Couville
   3 Eperlecques
   4 Lottinghen
   5 Mimoyecques
   6 Siracourt
   7 Sottevast
   8 Tamerville
   9 Wizernes

V1 Abteilung areas

▪ V1 Stellungssystem-I/II [old 'ski' site]
▪ V1 Stellungssystem-III [old 'ski' site]
▴ V1 operational site system [new 'modified' site]

British airfields 1 August 1944

■ London
1   Bradwell Bay [No. 219 Sqn RAF]
2   Brenzett [Nos 129, 306 & 315 Sqns RAF]
3   Castle Camps [No. 68 Sqn RAF]
4   Coltishall [No. 316 Sqn RAF]
5   Deanland [Nos 91 & 322 Sqns RAF]
6   Ford [No. 96 Sqn RAF; No. 456 Sqn RAAF]
7   Friston [No. 610 Sqn RAF]
8   Lympne [Nos 1 & 41 Sqns RAF]
9   Manston [No. 616 Sqn RAF]
10 Middle Wallop [No. 125 Sqn RAF;
    No. 418 Sqn RCAF]
11 Newchurch [Nos 3 & 56 Sqns RAF;
    No. 486 Sqn RNZAF]
12 West Malling [Nos 85 & 157 Sqns RAF]
13 Wittering [Fighter Interception Unit]

'Diver' AAA belt
Balloon barrage
Allied frontline
1 August 1944

An He 111H-16 of KG 53 waits for darkness before setting out across the North Sea to air-launch its V1 against London. It was aircraft such as this one that flew the last He 111 bomber sorties of the air war in the west. (John Weal)

launched, and of those 404 were shot down – 320 by AAA, 73 by the RAF and 11 by the Royal Navy. Only 388 impacted England, with just 66 reaching London.

As the airborne launching campaign came to an end, the last phase of the V1 bombardment against London was about to begin. In February, the new extended-range Fi 103E-1 entered service. With the weapon boasting the ability to reach London from the Netherlands, 21 sites were prepared for Operation *Pappdeckel* (Pasteboard). The attacks commenced on 3 March when 275 missiles were fired at London. As mentioned earlier, the Meteor IIIs of No. 616 Sqn were called upon to help in the defence of the capital, but they failed to down any V1s. By 29 March it was all over, the sites having been overrun by Allied troops. Of the 275 V1s launched, only about 160 flew any significant distance. Some 92 were shot down, and only 13 reached London. The world's first guided missile attack was finally over.

The greatest strength of the V1 was its simplicity and cheapness, while its greatest weakness was its inaccuracy (a major source of error was the wind). In Phase I of the aerial bombardment, 86 per cent of bombs successfully launched landed within 30 miles of the centre of the target. In Phase II only 64 per cent of the air-launched bombs landed within 30 miles of the target, and in the final phase 93 per cent of the ground-launched Fi 103E-1s fired from Holland fell within 30 miles of London.

The damage to the capital had been extensive. A total of 6,139 civilians and service personnel were killed, with 17,238 seriously injured and close to a million structures damaged. As a unit, *Flak-Regiment* 155(W) had just 189 men killed, 71 posted missing and 321 wounded – more than 10 per cent of the casualties were caused by launching accidents. ADGB suffered 72 pilots/navigators killed in action against the V1, many of them perishing when their target detonated in mid-air. Others were shot down in error by British or American AAA. A total of 2,900 Allied airmen were also lost during the *Crossbow* campaign and subsequent bombing raids against V-weapon launch and production sites.

The V1 bombardment of London came to an end on 29 March 1945. Approximately 10,500 Fi 103s had been launched against England. Of those, 5,890 crossed the coast. A grand total of 4,261 were destroyed by the defences (40 V1s were shot down by USAAF fighters, but they do not appear to have been included in the official figures). Official figures credit ADGB fighters with a total of 1,902 V1s destroyed up to the end of August 1944, but the figure should be closer to 2,250 according to the extensively researched book *Diver! Diver! Diver!* by Brian Cull and Bruce Lander. Land-based AAA guns brought down a further 1,971, gun batteries on Royal Navy vessels claimed 33 and barrage balloons destroyed 278.

In the end, the title of most effective V1 killer in ADGB went to the Tempest V with 851.75 kills. This was followed by various Mosquito nightfighter variants with 586.5, the Spitfire F XIV with 377.333, the Mustang III with 246.5 and the Spitfire F IX with 116.25 V1s shot down.

AFTERMATH

The results of the campaign were greatly in the enemy's favour, the estimated ratio of our costs to his being nearly four-to-one.
Air Ministry report, 4 November 1944

The V1 was a paradox of failure and unintended success. As an area bombardment weapon (with a target the size of London), it was a masterpiece of simplicity and economics. When it came to strictly military targets the V1 was useless. As hoped by Hitler, it did not spread the terror and panic he believed would force the British government to the negotiation table. Its real success lay in the amount of resources that had to be diverted in order to defeat the threat. Fortunately for the Allies they had complete air superiority, and a healthy amount of reserves in terms of fighter squadrons and AAA defences. They could also deploy these forces without affecting their overall plan for D-Day and beyond.

The V1 programme also cost the Germans dearly. By June 1944 the only two arms of the Wehrmacht that still had any impact on the battlefield were the Panzer/infantry divisions and the well-organised flak regiments. Both of these entities needed fuel and ammunition. The V1 programme siphoned off an immense amount of fuel (Allied estimates stated that 10,000 V1s used 133 gallons per missile, for an overall fuel burn of 1,331,200 gallons) that could have been used by its ground forces to good effect. The V1s also consumed nearly half the total explosive usage of the entire Wehrmacht in the critical months of July, August and September 1944. The result was that rock salt had to be substituted as an extender in artillery shells, making them less effective.

In the end, whether the V1 had been used or not, the outcome of the war would have been the same. The Allies' material superiority and the huge Soviet Red Army in the east, which destroyed the bulk of the Wehrmacht, meant that the Third Reich was

A B-17G from the 2754th Experimental Wing climbs away from Holloman Air Force Base, New Mexico, during a JB-2 'Thunderbug' test flight in the late 1940s. From October 1944 to 1949 the USAAF tested both their ground and air-launched copies of the V1. Unfortunately, it ran into the same problems the Luftwaffe had, forcing the abandonment of the JB-2 programme owing to poor accuracy and pulse-jet performance limitations. (NARA)

moving inexorably towards defeat. It was only a question of how long would it take. But even in failure the Allies were impressed.

Just as the Germans had produced their own version of the British Sten submachine gun, the Americans decided to make their own 'Chinese copy' (Republic-Ford JB-2 Loon) of the V1. What had impressed the Allies the most was the cost-effectiveness of the weapon. The Allies knew that air power was vital for success on land and over the sea, but achieving this was expensive both in terms of manpower and machinery. In late July 1944, the USAAF ordered 1,000 JB-2s, with Republic and Willys building the airframe and Ford the engine. The programme was finally cancelled in September 1945. Both the Soviets and the French built their own copies of the V1, with the former abandoning the programme in 1951 and the latter producing a target drone version for air-to-air missile tests.

The Gloster Meteor had a much brighter future. While a mediocre performer when compared with the Me 262 in the last few months of the war, it would prove a Cold War stalwart. In time airframe refinements and more powerful engines would produce the Meteor F 8 interceptor, which equipped no fewer than 31 RAF and Royal Auxiliary Air Force squadrons. In numerical terms, the Meteor F 8 was produced in the greatest volume – 1,183 examples. The fighter was also an export success, with hundreds being sold to Argentina, Australia, Denmark, Belgium, Brazil, Denmark, Ecuador, Egypt, Israel, West Germany, Netherlands, South Africa, Syria and Sweden. In total 3,545 Meteors and Meteor nightfighters were built.

Another six years would pass before the Meteor again battled another jet-powered aircraft. That honour fell to No. 77 Sqn of the Royal Australian Air Force (RAAF) during the Korean War. Equipped with Meteor F 8s, the Australian pilots had high hopes that their new mounts (the jets had replaced Mustangs) could handle the Soviet-built MiG-15. In terms of performance, however, the Meteor was at a distinct disadvantage when compared with the swept-wing MiG. On 29 August 1951 that weakness was cruelly revealed when eight Meteors clashed with six MiG-15s. The RAAF lost one Meteor and had two more badly damaged, while the communists suffered no losses. Finally, on 1 December that same year, Flg Off Bruce Gogerly (flying A77-15) claimed No. 77 Sqn's first MiG-15 victory during a clash that had seen the unit engage approximately 40 enemy jets. Two MiG-15s were destroyed, but it was a bittersweet victory for three Meteors were downed. By the end of the war No. 77 Sqn had flown 4,836 sorties in the Meteor F 8 and destroyed six MiG-15s.

Today, two Gloster Meteor T 7 two-seat trainers remain in service in the UK, WL419 and WA638 being used as flying test beds for the world-famous Martin-Baker ejection seat company.

Two RAAF Meteor F 8s of No. 77 Sqn are seen parked in their sand-bagged revetment at K-14 Kimpo airfield, near Seoul, during the Korean War. A77-368, on the left, served with the unit from July 1951 to August 1953. In total, the aircraft flew no fewer than 485 operational missions, the vast majority of them in the ground attack role. On 3 November 1951, while piloted by Sgt M. E. Colebrook DFM USAF, it was credited with damaging a MiG-15 in combat. (National Museum of the United States Air Force)

FURTHER READING

Basil, Collier, *The Battle of the V-Weapons 1944–45* (London: Hodder & Stoughton, 1964)

Bowyer, Michael, *Fighting Colours – RAF Fighter Camouflage and Markings 1937–1975* (Cambridge: Patrick Stephens, 1975)

Brown, Capt Eric, CBE, DSC, AFC, RN, *Wings of Weird and the Wonderful* (Manchester: Hikoki Publications, 2010)

Cull, Brian, *Diver! Diver! Diver! RAF and American Fighter Pilots Battle the V1 Assault over Southeast England 1944–45* (London: Grub Street, 2008)

Dobinson, Colin, *AA Command – Britain's Anti-Aircraft Defences of the Second World War* (London: Methuen, 2001)

Ethell, Jeffrey L., *World War II Fighting Jets* (Annapolis, MD: Airlife, 1994)

Friedrich, Georg, *Hitler's Miracle Weapons – the secret of the rockets and flying craft of the Third Reich. Vol. 1, From the V1 to the A9* (Solihull: Helion, 2004)

Goulding, James and Robert Jones, *Camouflage & Markings RAF Fighter Command Northern Europe 1936 to 1945* (London: Ducimus Books Ltd, 1971)

James, Derek N., *Gloster Aircraft Since 1917* (London: Putnam, 1971)

Johnson, Brian, *The Secret War* (London: British Broadcasting Corporation, 1978)

Johnson, David, *V1 & V2 – Hitler's Vengeance on London* (New York, NY: Stein & Day, 1992)

Joachim, Engelmann, *V1 – The Flying Bomb* (Atglen, PA: Schiffer, 1992)

Mason, Tim, *The Secret Years – Flight Testing at Boscombe Down 1939–1945* (Manchester: Hikoki Publications, 2010)

Nijboer, Donald, *Graphic War – The Secret Aviation Drawings and Illustrations of World War II* (Erin: The Boston Mills Press, 2005)

Ogley, Bob, *Doodle Bugs and Rockets – The Battle of the Flying Bombs* (Kent: Froglets Publications, 1992)

Price, Dr Alfred, *The Last Year of the Luftwaffe – May 1944 to May 1945* (Osceola, WI: Motorbooks, 1991)

Price, Dr Alfred, *The Luftwaffe Data Book* (Mechanicsburg, PA: Greenhill Books/Stackpole, 1997)

Pitchfork, Graham, *The RAF's First Jet Squadron – 616 South Yorkshire* (Stroud: The History Press, 2009)

Pitchfork, Graham, 'No 616 Sqn – first in Jets', *JETS* magazine, Spring 1999 edition, pp. 49–55

Roy, Irons, *Hitler's Terror Weapons – The Price of Vengeance* (London: Collins, 2002)

Shacklady, Edward, *The Gloster Meteor* (London: Macdonald, 1962)

Shores, Christopher F. and Williams, Clive, *Aces High – The Fighter Aces of the British and Commonwealth Air Forces in World War II* (London: Grub Street, 1994)

Shores, Christopher F., *Aces High Vol. 2* (London: Grub Street, 1999)

Shores, Christopher F. and Thomas, Chris, *2nd Tactical Air Force Vol. I* (Crowborough: Classic Publications, 2004)

Shores, Christopher and Thomas, Chris, *2nd Tactical Air Force Vol. III* (Crowborough: Classic Publications, 2006)

Shores, Christopher and Thomas, Chris, *2nd Tactical Air Force Vol. IV* (Crowborough: Classic Publications, 2008)

Westermann, Edward B., *Flak German Anti-Aircraft Defences, 1914 to 1945* (Lawrence, KS: University Press of Kansas, 2001)

Williamson, Murray, *The Luftwaffe 1933-45 – Strategy for Defeat* (Maxwell AFB, AL: Brasseys, 1996)

Zaloga, Steven J., *New Vanguard 106 – V-1 Flying Bomb 1942–52: Hitler's Infamous "Doodlebug"* (Oxford: Osprey Publishing, 2005)

Zaloga, Steven J., *Fortress 72 – German V-Weapons Sites 1943–45* (Oxford: Osprey Publishing, 2008)

INDEX